The Sensational Guitar Songbook

ISBN 978-1-4234-7781-5

HAL•LEONARD®
CORPORATION

7777 W. BLUEMOUND RD. P.O. BOX 13819 MILWAUKEE, WI 53213

Visit Hal Leonard Online at
www.halleonard.com

The Sensational Guitar Songbook

Barracuda

Words and Music by Nancy Wilson, Ann Wilson, Michael Derosier and Roger Fisher

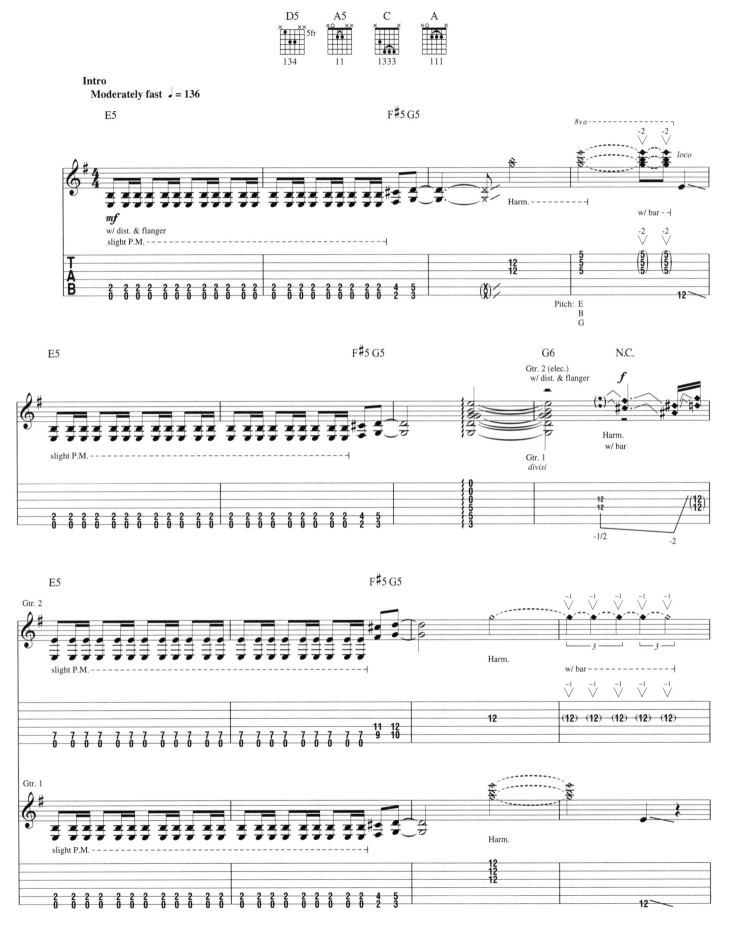

*Chord symbols reflect overall harmony.

bet you gon - na am - bush ___ me. _____
make up some - thing ___ quick. _____

You'd have me down, _ down, _ down, _____
You gon - na burn, _ burn, _ burn, _____

slight P.M. - - - - - - - -|

slight P.M. - - - - - - - -|

*See top of first page of song for chord diagrams
pertaining to rhythm slashes.

To Coda 1 ✛   *To Coda 2* ✛

Gtr. 3 tacet
3rd time, Gtrs. 1 & 2: w/ Rhy. Fills 3 & 3A
N.C.

_ down on my _____ knees, _____ now would - n't ya, bar - ra - cu -
_ burn, burn it to the wick.

Rhy. Fill 3
Gtr. 1

fdbk.   w/ bar

Pitch: F#   -1

Rhy. Fill 3A
Gtr. 2

Harm.
w/ bar

-1

7

Interlude

D.S. al Coda 1

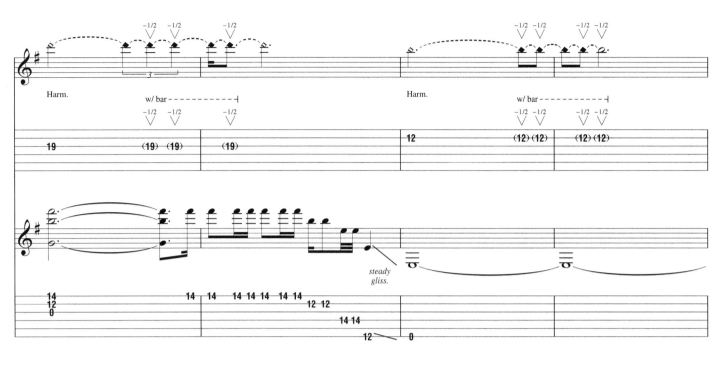

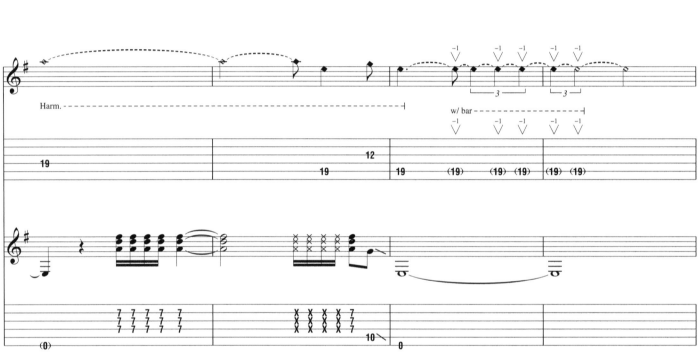

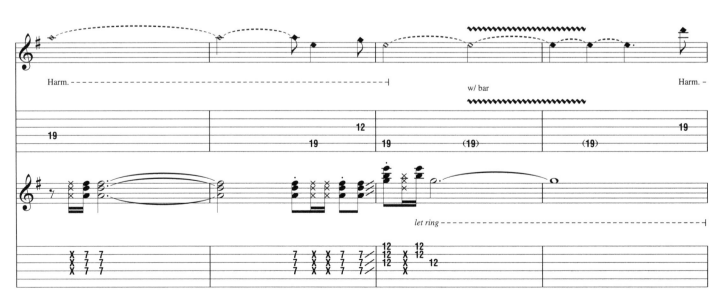

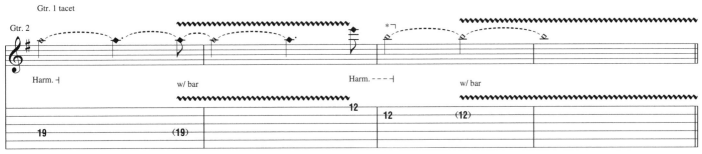

*Played behind the beat.

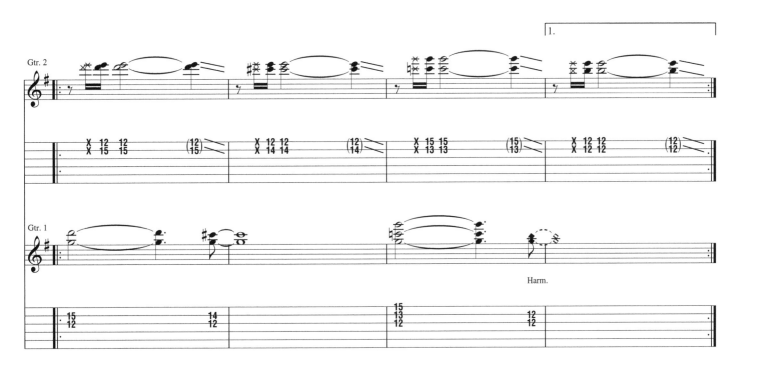

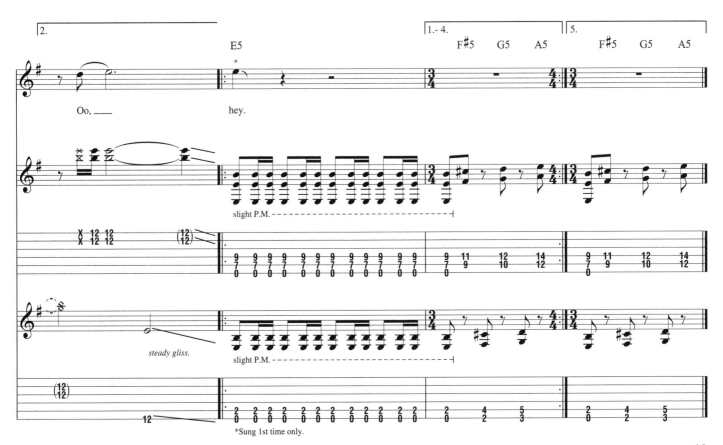

*Sung 1st time only.

It's Not Over

Words and Music by Chris Daughtry, Gregg Wattenberg, Mark Wilkerson and Brett Young

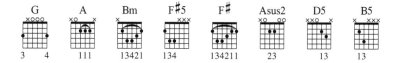

Gtrs. 1 & 4-7: Tune down 1/2 step:
(low to high) E♭-A♭-D♭-G♭-B♭-E♭

Gtrs. 2 & 3: Drop D tuning, down 1/2 step:
(low to high) D♭-A♭-D♭-G♭-B♭-E♭

Verse
Slowly ♩ = 73

*Chord symbols reflect implied harmony.

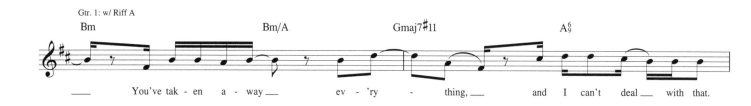

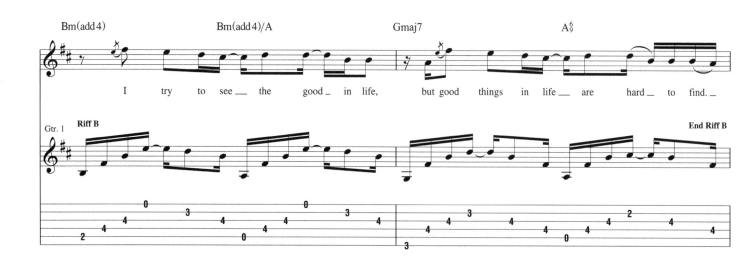

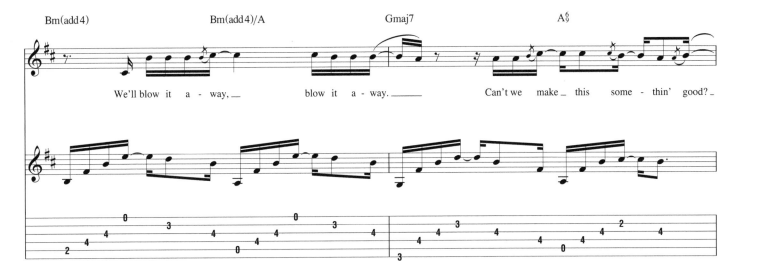

We'll blow it a - way, __ blow it a - way. __ Can't we make __ this some - thin' good? __

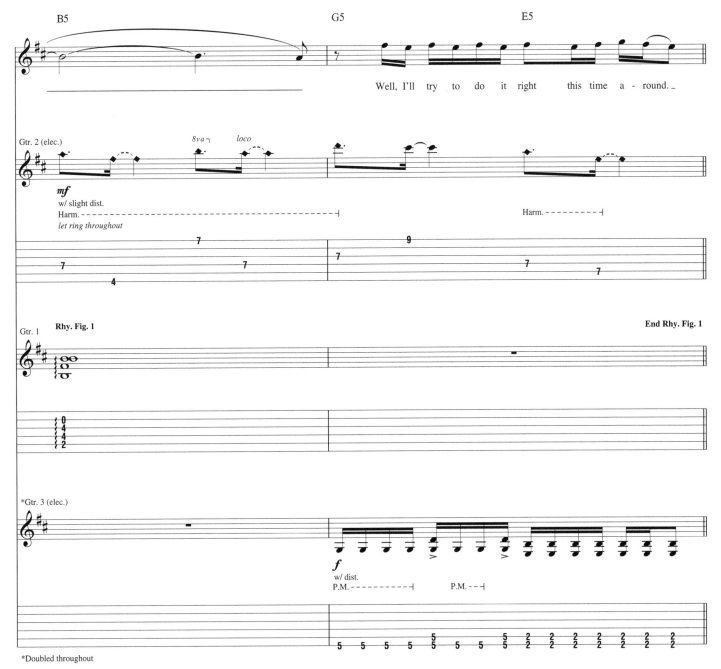

Well, I'll try to do it right this time a - round. __

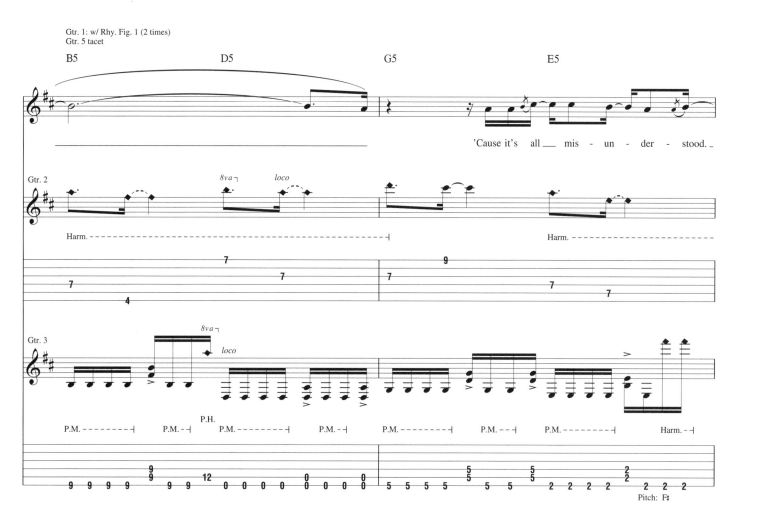

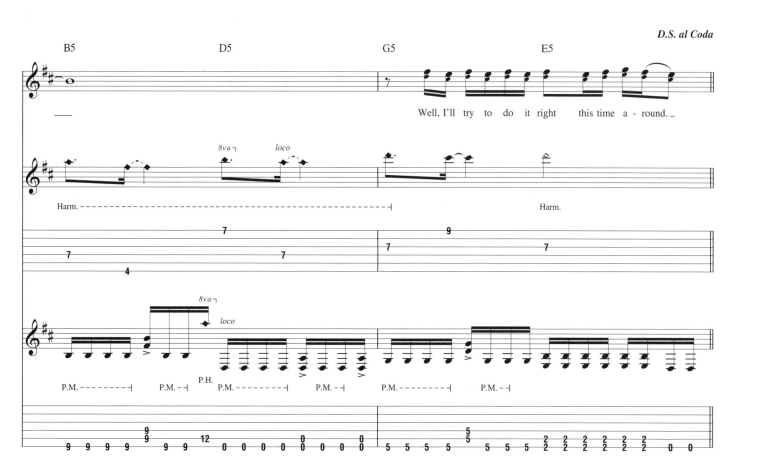

⊕ Coda

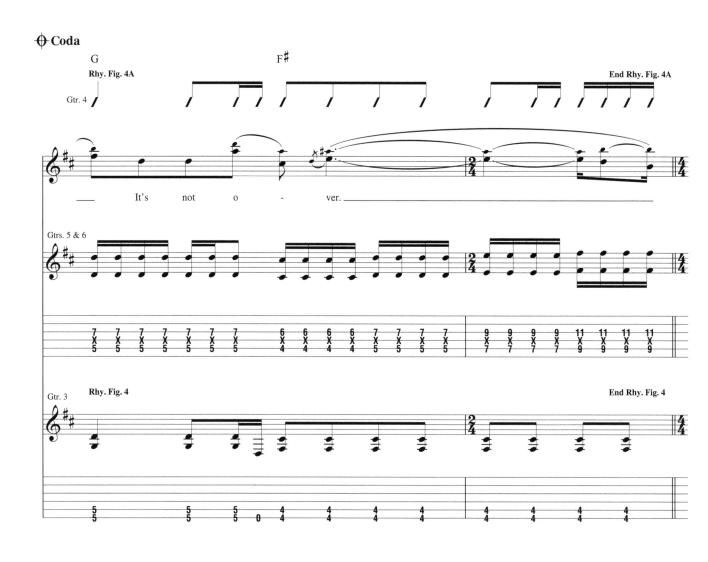

It's not o - ver.

Guitar Solo

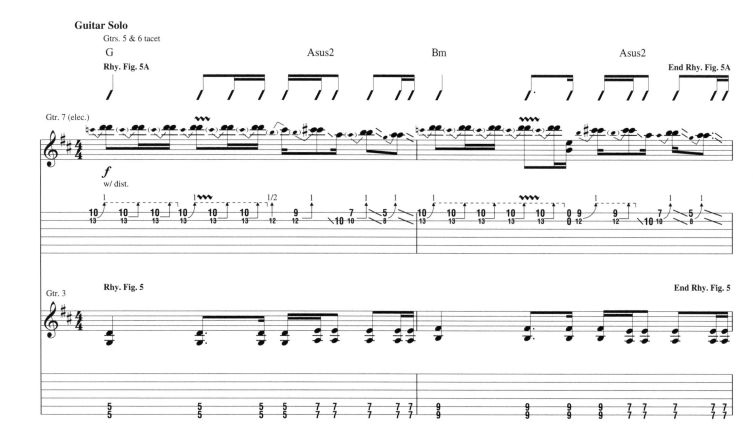

Bridge

Gtrs. 3 & 4: w/ Rhy. Figs. 5 & 5A
Gtr. 7 tacet

Gtrs. 3 & 4: w/ Rhy. Figs. 4 & 4A

Chorus

Gtrs. 3 & 4: w/ Rhy. Figs. 2 & 2A (1st 3 meas.)
Gtrs. 5 & 6: w/ Riffs C & C1 (1st 3 meas.)

Gtr. 6: w/ Riff C1 (1st meas., 2 times)

Outro-Chorus

Gtrs. 3 & 4: w/ Rhy. Figs. 2 & 2A
Gtr. 5: w/ Riff C
Gtr. 6: w/ Riff C1 (1st meas., 3 times)

22

23

Peggy Sue

from THE BUDDY HOLLY STORY

Words and Music by Jerry Allison, Norman Petty and Buddy Holly

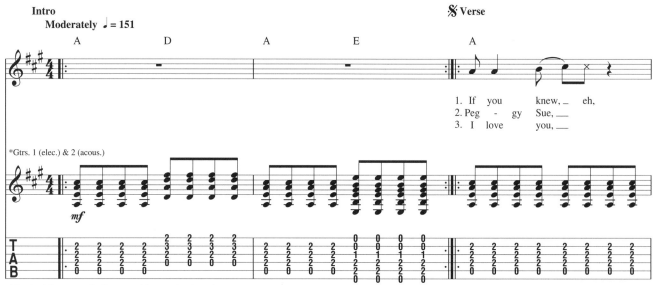

*Gtr. 1 w/ clean tone. Gtr. 2 strums w/ downstrokes throughout.
Composite arrangement

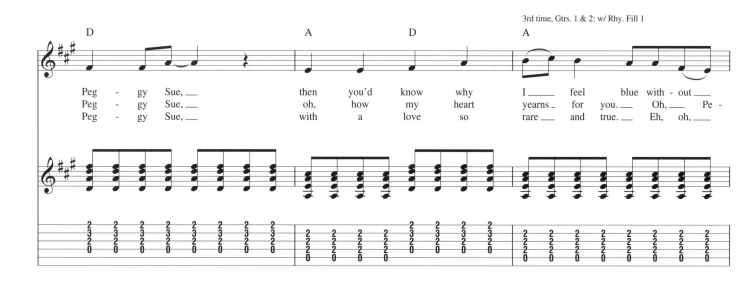

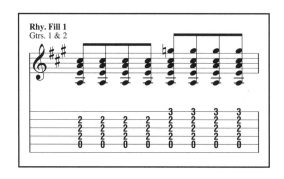

Plush

Words and Music by Scott Weiland, Dean DeLeo, Robert DeLeo and Eric Kretz

*Chord symbols reflect implied harmony.

**Gtr. 2 (slight dist.) played *mf*.
Composite arrangement

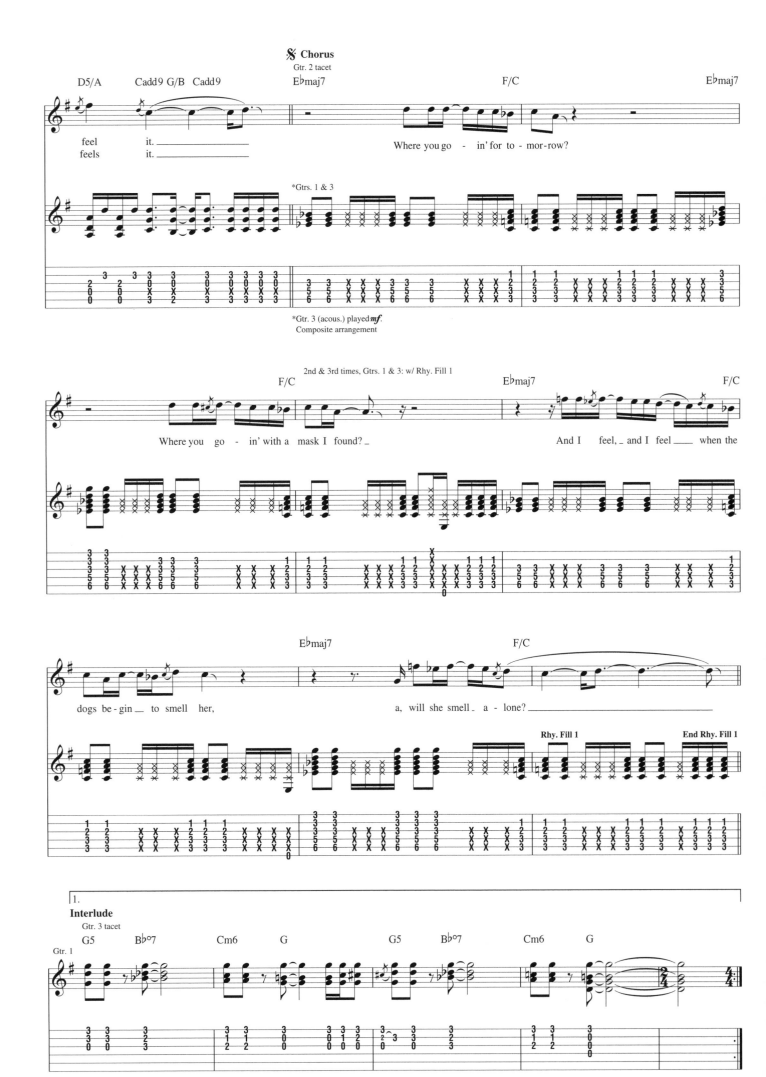

Interlude
A tempo

D.S. al Coda
(take 2nd ending)

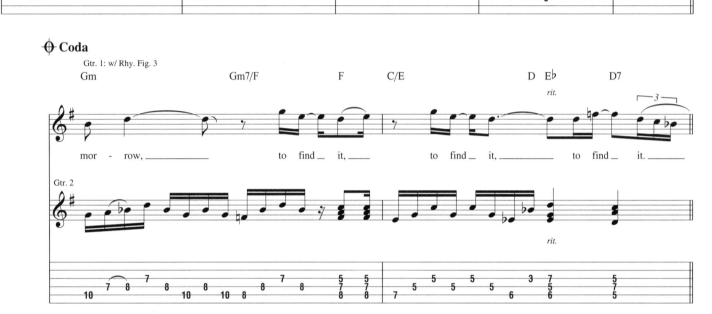

Coda

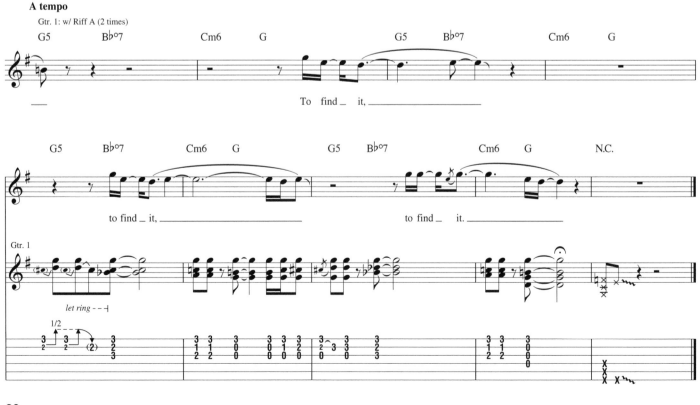

Outro
A tempo

Rock of Ages

Words and Music by Joe Elliott, Richard Savage, Richard Allen, Steve Clark, Peter Willis and R.J. Lange

gim - me, gim - me, gim - me, gim - me one more — for the road, — yeah.

Pitch: E   F#

Bridge

Gtrs. 1 & 3: w/ Rhy. Fig. 2

A5   G5   N.C.   A5   G5   N.C.   E5   G5 A5

What _ do _ you want? _____   I _____ want _ rock 'n' roll. _

What do you want? _

Guitar Solo

N.C.   A5   E5   E5 N.C.

You bet ya!

Long _ live _ rock 'n' roll. _   Ah, yes!

Gtr. 4 (dist.)

mf

Pitch: F#

Pitch: G
D

Run to the Hills

Words and Music by Steven Harris

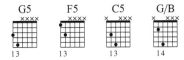

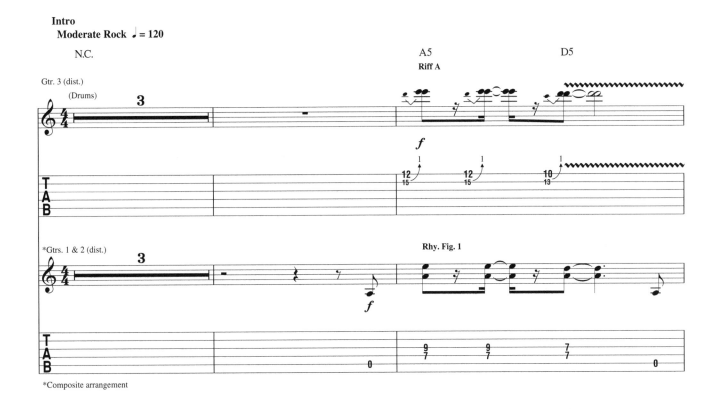

*Composite arrangement

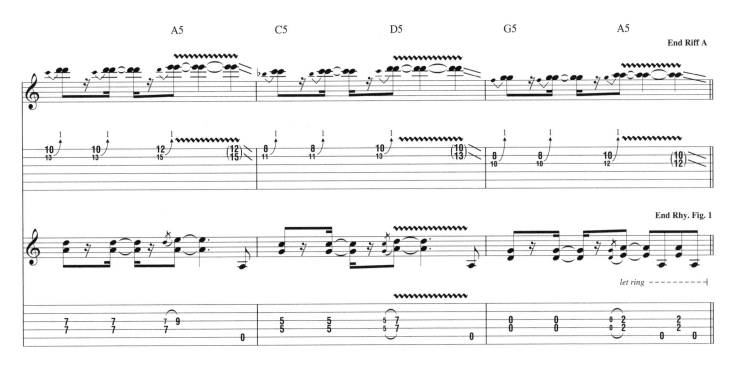

Verse

Gtrs. 1 & 2: w/ Rhy. Fig. 1 (3 3/4 times)
Gtr. 3: w/ Riff A (3 3/4 times)

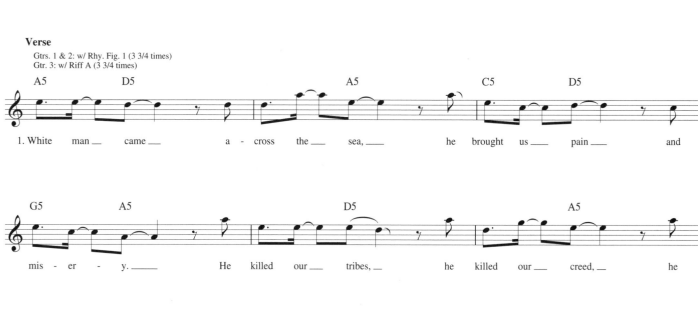

A5　　　D5　　　　　　　　　A5　　　　　　C5　　　D5

1. White man ___ came ___ a - cross the ___ sea, ___ he brought us ___ pain ___ and

G5　　　　A5　　　　　　　　　D5　　　　　　　A5

mis - er - y. ___ He killed our ___ tribes, ___ he killed our ___ creed, ___ he

C5　　　D5　　　　G5　　　A5　　　　　　　D5

took our ___ game ___ for his own ___ need. ___ We fought him ___ hard, ___ we

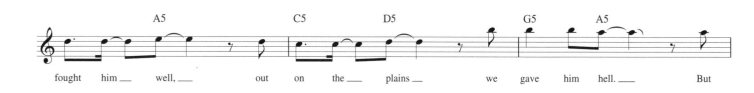

A5　　　　　C5　　　D5　　　　　G5　　A5

fought him ___ well, ___ out on the ___ plains ___ we gave him hell. ___ But

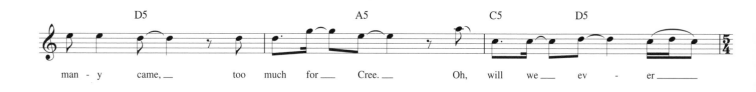

D5　　　　　　　　　A5　　　　　　C5　　　D5　　　5/4

man - y came, ___ too much for ___ Cree. ___ Oh, will we ___ ev - er ___

Interlude

Faster ♩ = 180

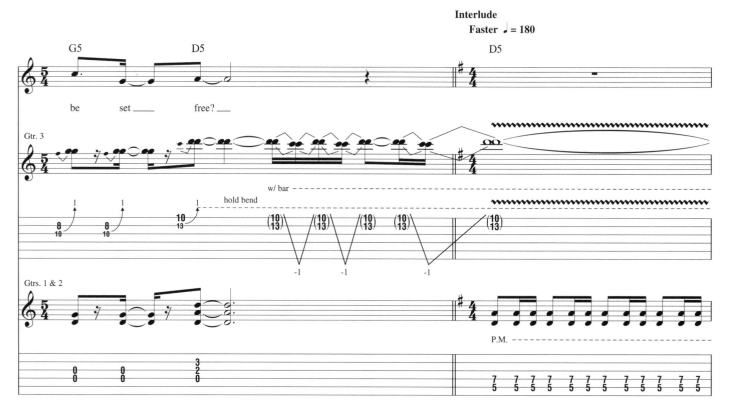

G5　　　　　D5　　　　　　　　　D5

be set ___ free? ___

Gtr. 3

w/ bar - - - - - - - - - - - - - - -
hold bend

Gtrs. 1 & 2

P.M. -

Verse

1st time, Gtr. 3 tacet

2. Rid - ing through dust __ clouds and bar - ren wastes, __
3. Sol - dier blue ____ in the bar - ren wastes, __

gal - lop - ing hard on the plains. __   Chas - ing the red - skins
hunt - ing and kill - ing's a game. __   Rap - ing the wom - en and

back to their holes,   fight - ing them at their own game. __
wast - ing the men,   the on - ly good in - juns are tame. __

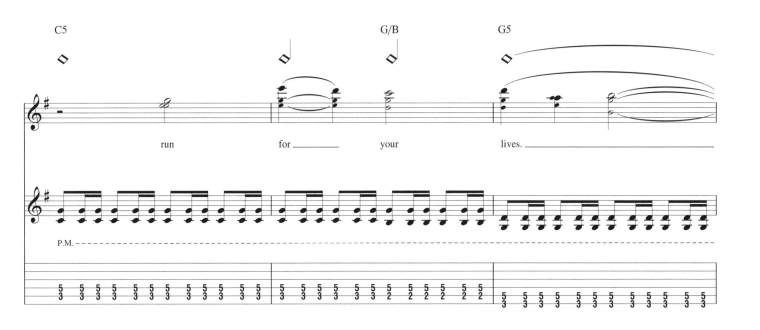

run   for _____   your   lives. _____

Gtrs. 1 & 2: w/ Rhy. Figs. 2 & 2A (1st 6 meas.)

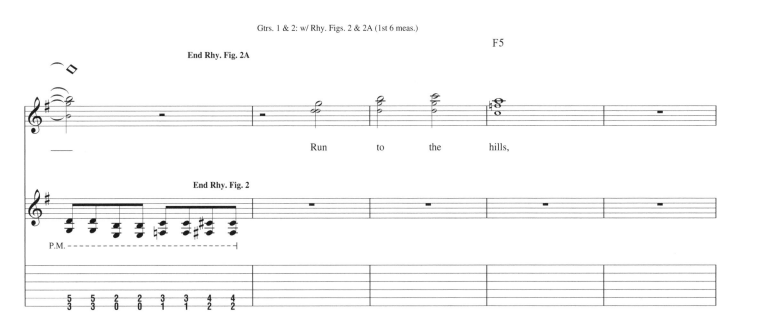

Run   to   the   hills,

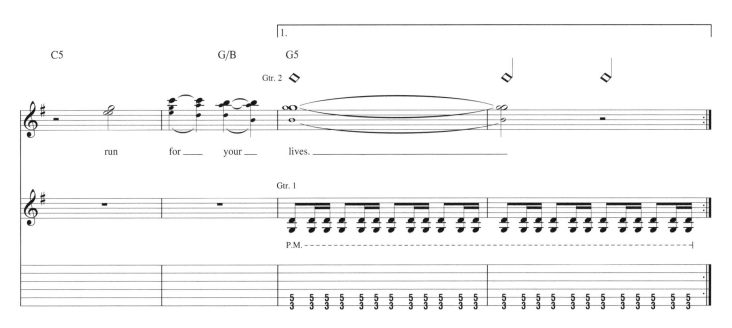

run   for ___ your ___ lives. ___

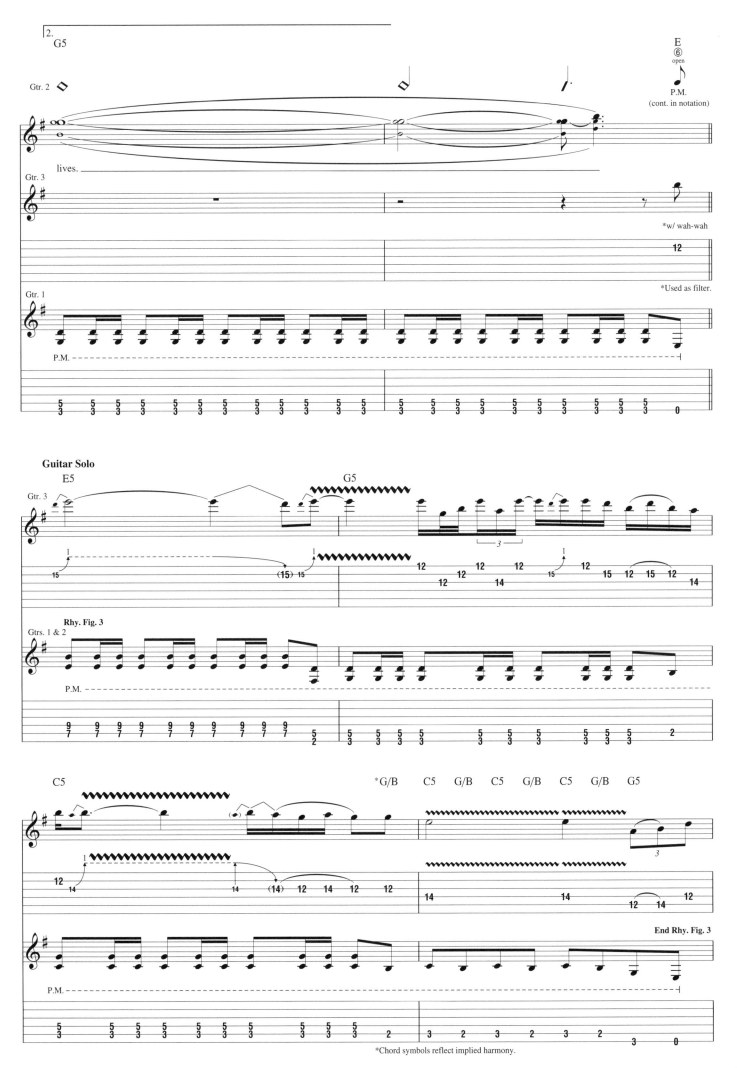

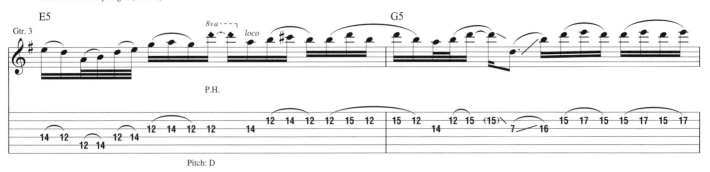

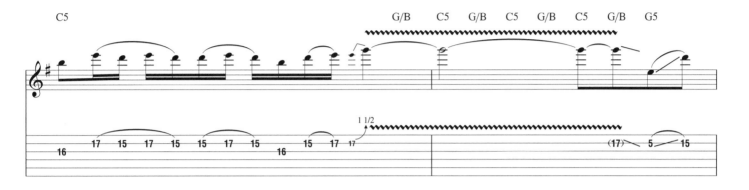

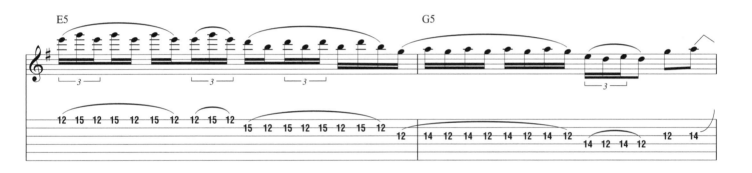

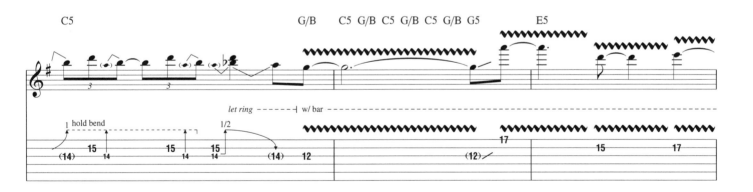

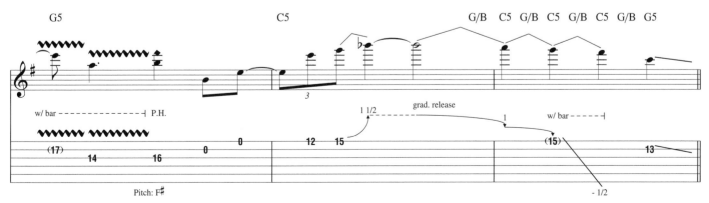

Interlude

1st time, Gtr. 3 tacet

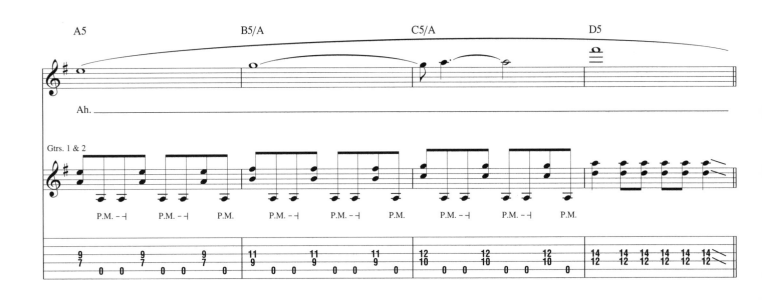

Outro-Chorus

Gtrs. 1 & 2: w/ Rhy. Figs. 2 & 2A (3 1/2 times)

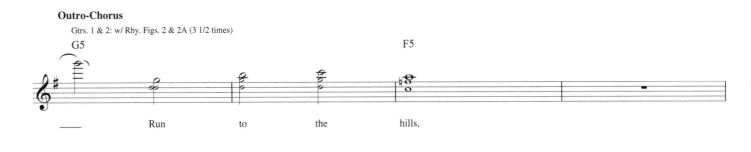

Run   to   the   hills,

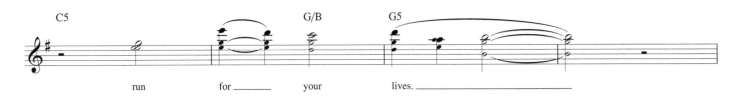

run   for _____ your   lives. _____

F5

Run   to   the   hills,

C5   G/B   G5

run   for _____   your _____   lives. _____

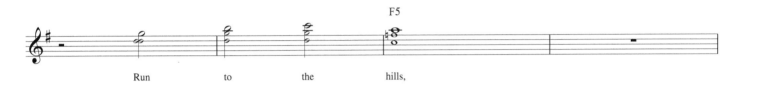

F5

Run   to   the   hills,

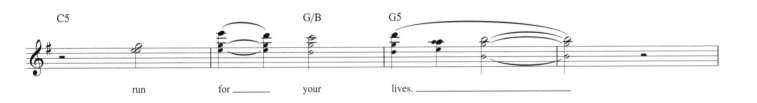

C5   G/B   G5

run   for _____   your   lives. _____

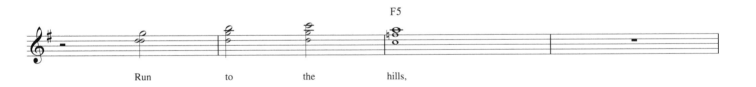

F5

Run   to   the   hills,

Free time

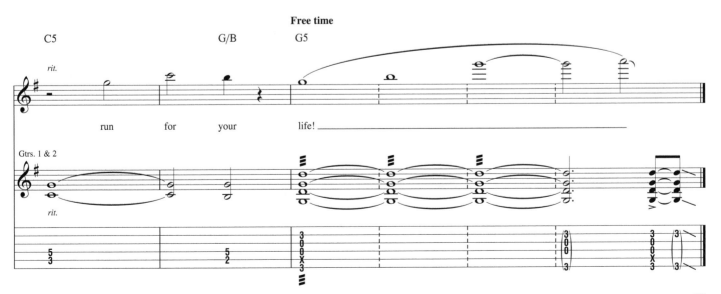

run   for   your   life! _____

Sex on Fire

Words and Music by Caleb Followill, Nathan Followill, Jared Followill and Matthew Followill

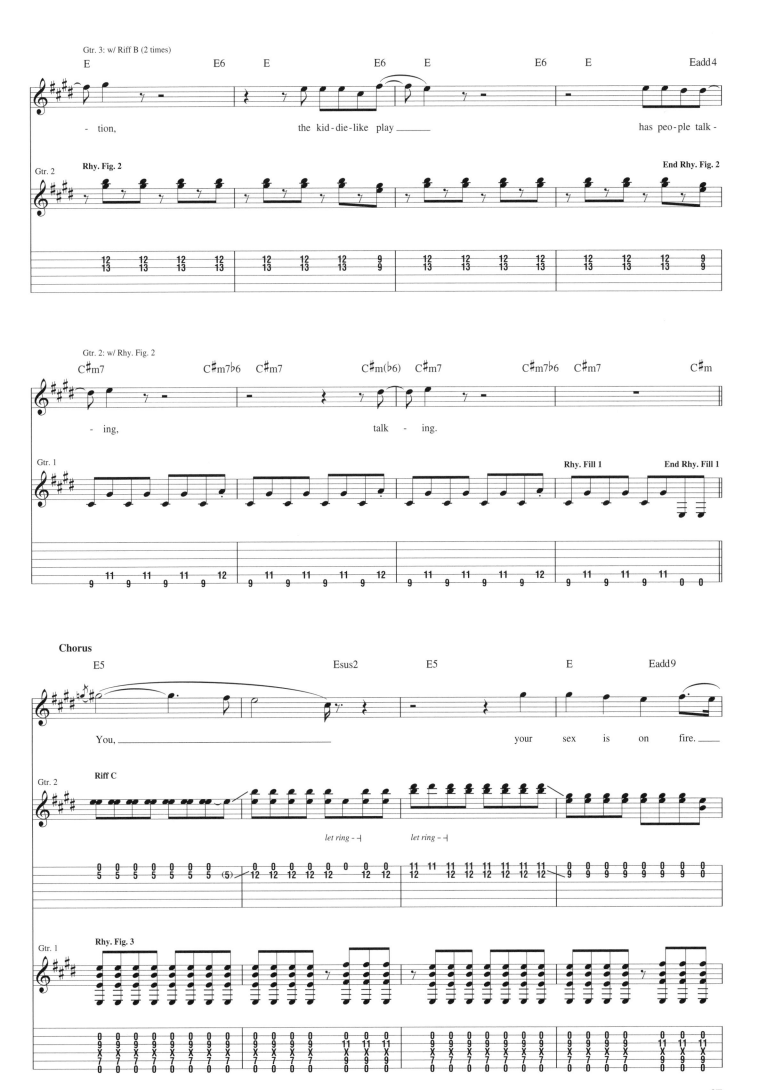

Chorus

Gtr. 1: w/ Rhy. Fig. 3 (1st 4 meas.)
1st time, Gtr. 2: w/ Riff C (1st 4 meas.)
2nd time, Gtr. 2: w/ Riff C

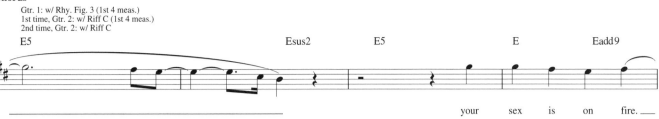

your sex is on fire.

To Coda ⊕

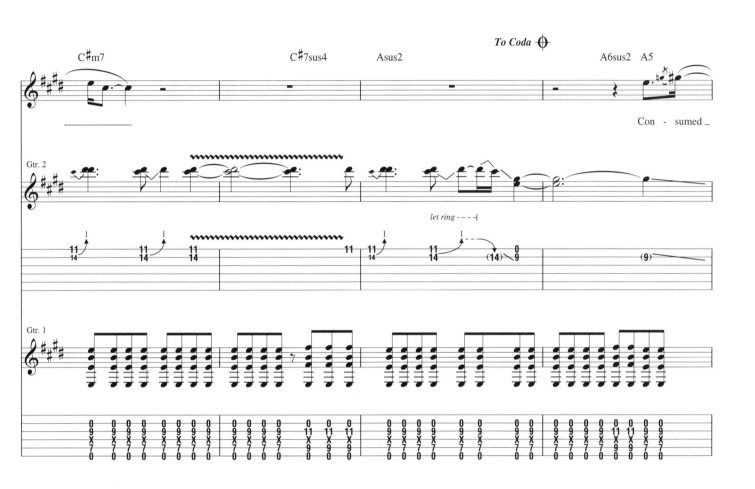

Con - sumed

Gtr. 1: w/ Rhy. Fig. 3
Gtr. 2: w/ Riff C (1st 4 meas.)

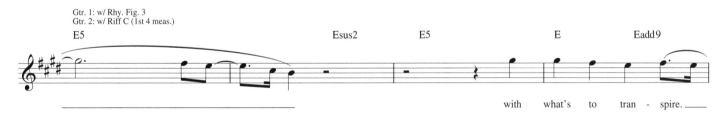

with what's to tran - spire.

D.S. al Coda

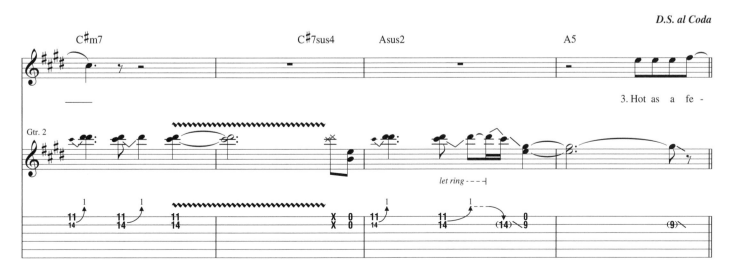

3. Hot as a fe -

⊕ **Coda**

Bad, Bad Leroy Brown

Words and Music by Jim Croce

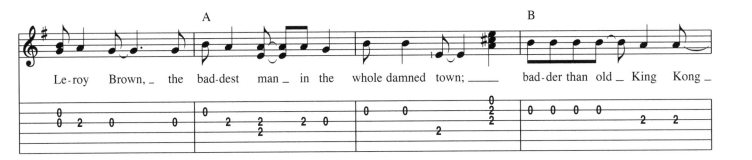

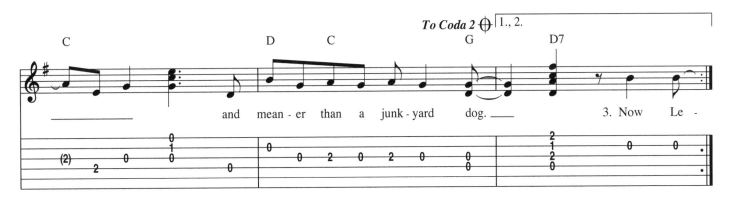

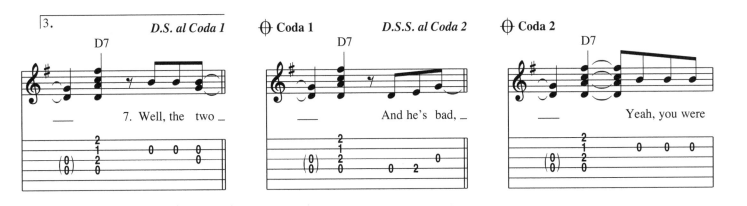

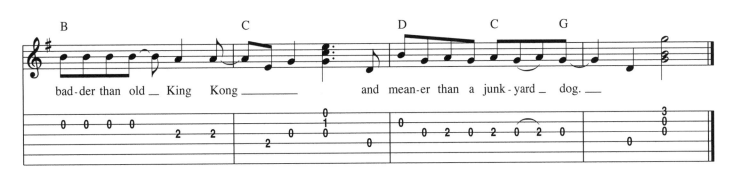

Additional Lyrics

3. Now Leroy, he a gambler
   And he like his fancy clothes
   And he like to wave
   His diamond rings
   In front of ev'rybody's nose.

4. He got a custom Continental,
   He got a Eldorado, too;
   He got a thirty-two gun
   In his pocket for fun,
   He's got a razor in his shoe.

5. Well, Friday 'bout a week ago,
   Leroy shootin' dice,
   And at the edge of the bar
   Sat a girl name of Doris,
   And oh, that girl looked nice.

6. Well, he cast his eyes upon her
   And the trouble soon began,
   And Leroy Brown,
   He learned a lesson 'bout messin'
   With the wife of a jealous man.

7. Well, the two men took to fightin',
   And when they pulled them from the floor
   Leroy looked
   Like a jigsaw puzzle
   With a couple of pieces gone.

Beer for My Horses

Words and Music by Toby Keith and Scott Emerick

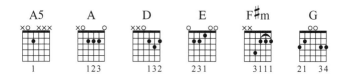

*Capo I

Strum Pattern: 1
Pick Pattern: 3

Intro
Moderately

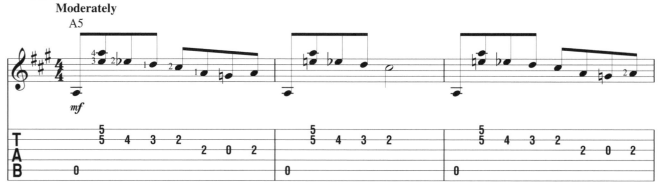

*Optional: To match recording, place capo at 1st fret.

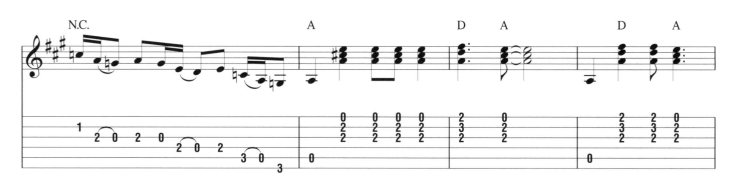

Verse

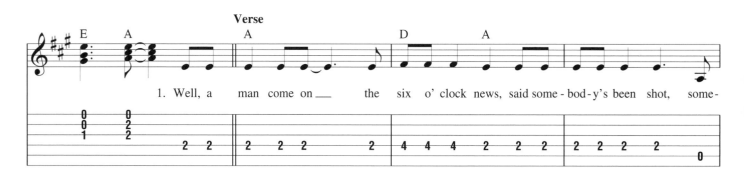

1. Well, a man come on __ the six o' clock news, said some-bod-y's been shot, some-

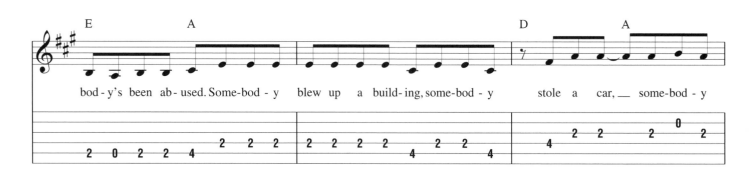

bod-y's been ab-used. Some-bod-y blew up a build-ing, some-bod-y stole a car, __ some-bod-y

got a - way, __ some-bod - y did-n't get too far, __ yeah.   They did - n't

E   A   F#m

E   A   **Verse**   A

get too far. __   2. Grand - pap - py told my pap - py, "Back in
                                   3. *See additional lyrics*

D   A   E   A

my day, son, __ a man had to an - swer for the wick - ed that he done." Take

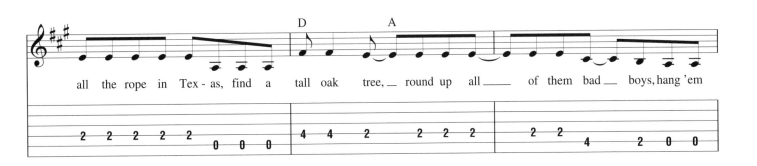

D   A

all the rope in Tex - as, find a tall oak tree, __ round up all ___ of them bad __ boys, hang 'em

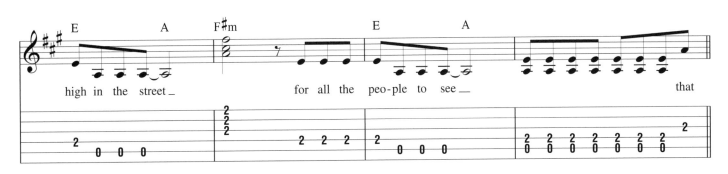

E   A   F#m   E   A

high in the street __   for all the peo-ple to see __   that

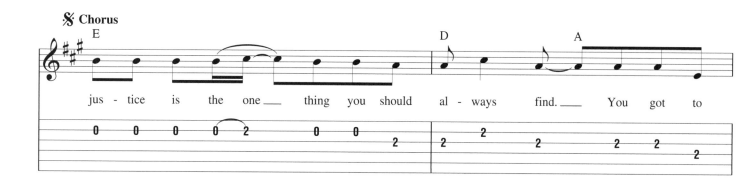

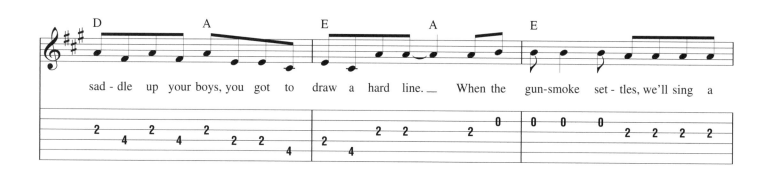

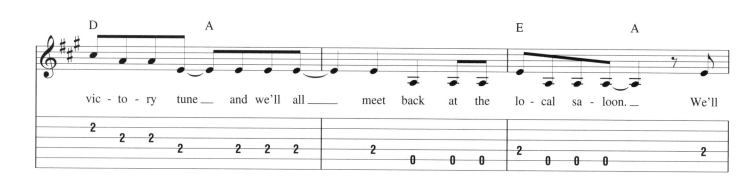

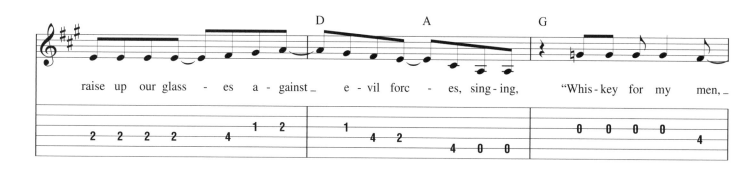

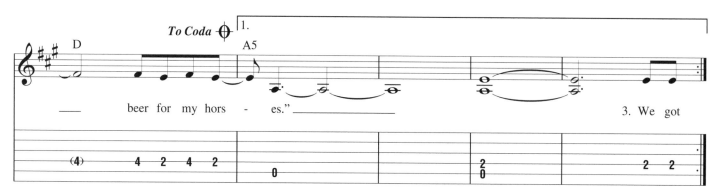

Additional Lyrics

3. We got too many gangsters doing dirty deeds,
Too much corruption and crime in the streets.
It's time the long arm of the law put a few more in the ground,
Send 'em all to their Maker and He'll settle 'em down.
You can bet He'll set 'em down, 'cause...

Black Hole Sun

Words and Music by Chris Cornell

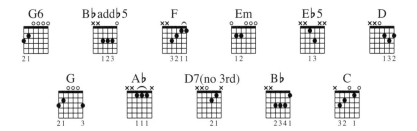

Strum Pattern: 3
Pick Pattern: 3

Verse

Slow Rock

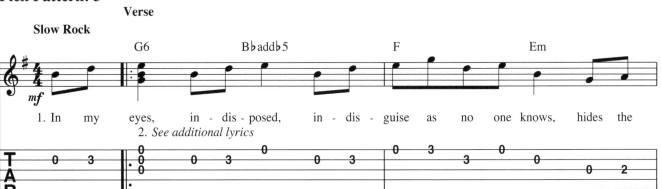

1. In my eyes, in - dis - posed, in - dis - guise as no one knows, hides the
2. *See additional lyrics*

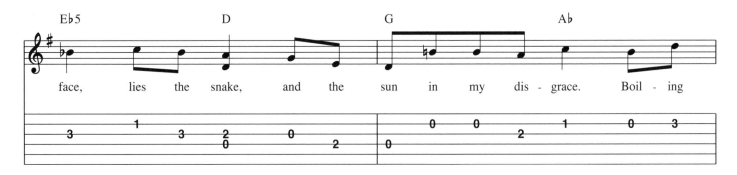

face, lies the snake, and the sun in my dis - grace. Boil - ing

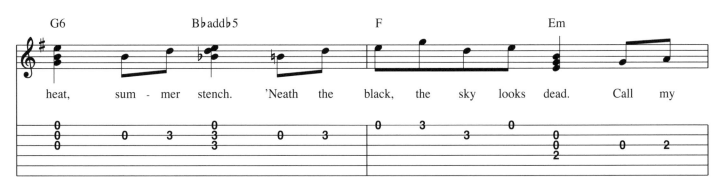

heat, sum - mer stench. 'Neath the black, the sky looks dead. Call my

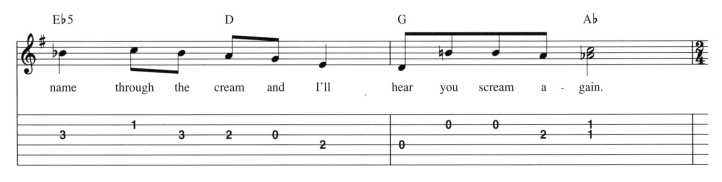

name through the cream and I'll hear you scream a - gain.

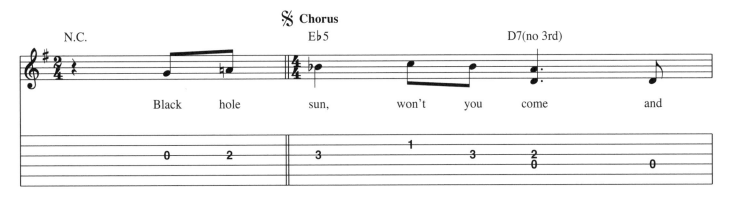

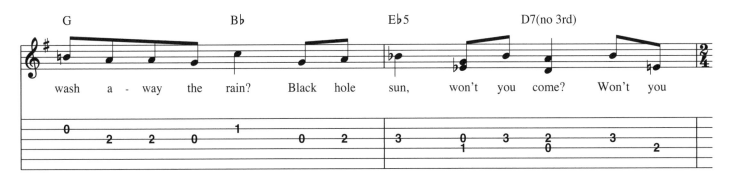

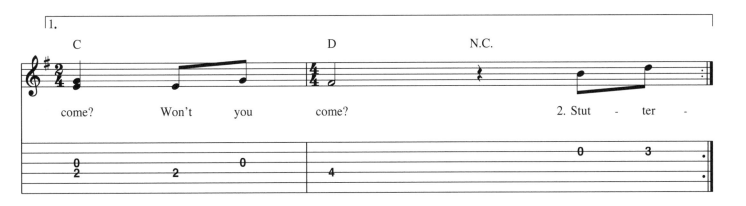

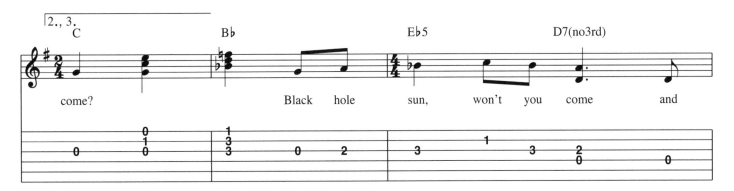

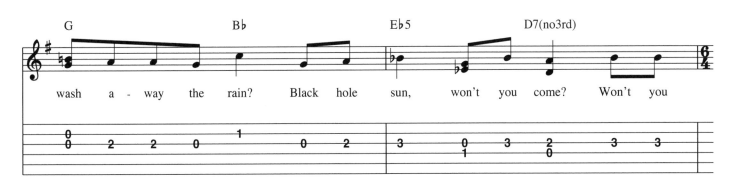

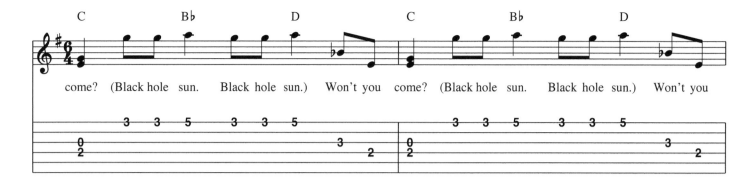

come? (Black hole sun. Black hole sun.) Won't you come? (Black hole sun. Black hole sun.) Won't you

To Coda ⊕

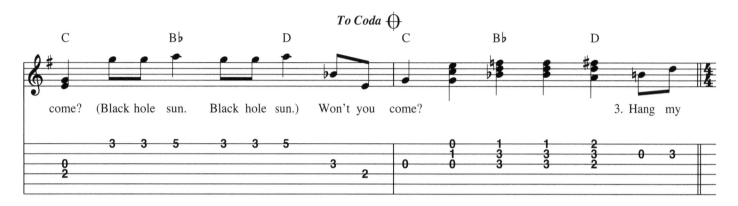

come? (Black hole sun. Black hole sun.) Won't you come? 3. Hang my

Verse

D.S. al Coda

head, drown my fear, till you all just dis - ap - pear. Black hole

⊕ **Coda**

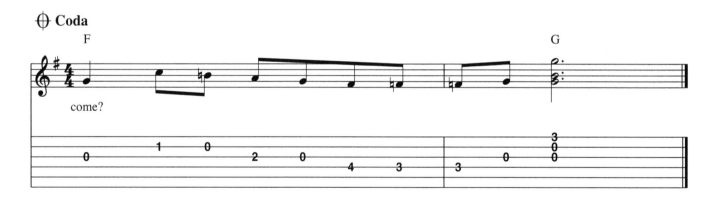

come?

Additional Lyrics

2. Stuttering, cold and damp.
   Steal the warm wind, tired friend.
   Times are gone for honest men,
   And sometimes far too long for snakes.
   In my shoes, a walking sleep.
   In my youth I pray to keep.
   Heaven send hell away.
   No one sings like you anymore.

Bubbly

Words and Music by Colbie Caillat and Jason Reeves

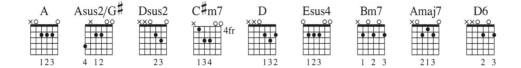

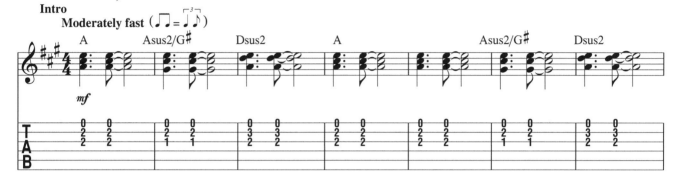

Strum Pattern: 4, 6
Pick Pattern: 4, 5

Intro
Moderately fast

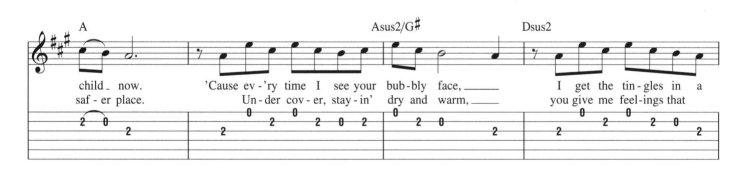

Verse

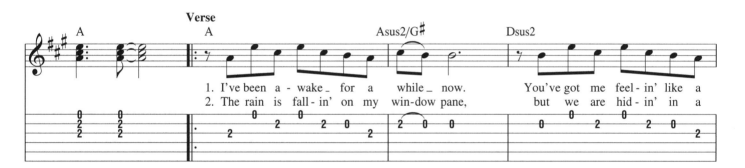

1. I've been a - wake_ for a while_ now. You've got me feel - in' like a
2. The rain is fall - in' on my win - dow pane, but we are hid - in' in a

child_ now. 'Cause ev - 'ry time I see your bub - bly face, ____ I get the tin - gles in a
saf - er place. Un - der cov - er, stay - in' dry and warm, ____ you give me feel - ings that

% Chorus

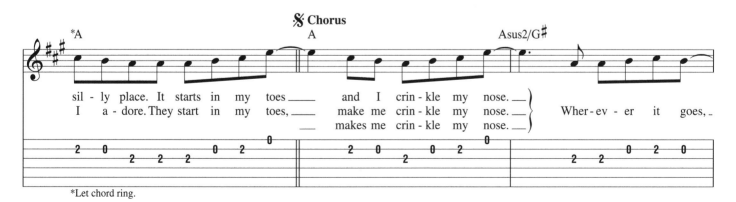

sil - ly place. It starts in my toes ____ and I crin - kle my nose. ____
I a - dore. They start in my toes, ____ make me crin - kle my nose. ____ Wher - ev - er it goes, _
____ makes me crin - kle my nose. ____

*Let chord ring.

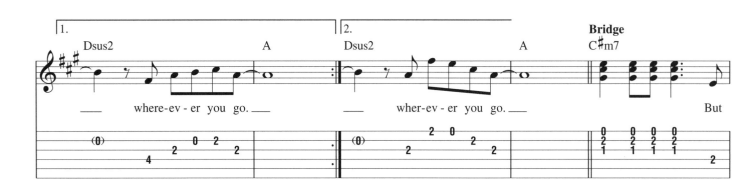

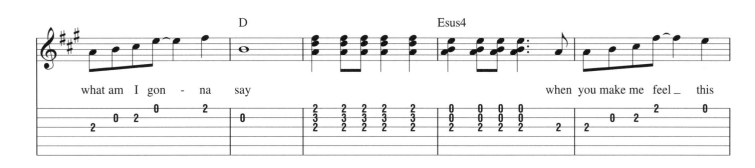

*Let chord ring.

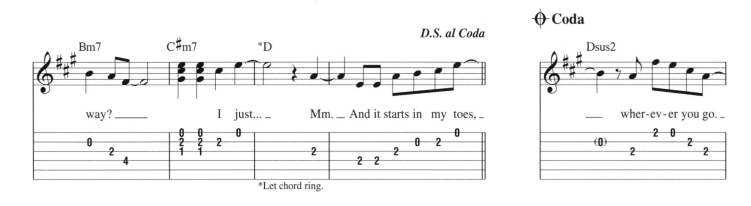

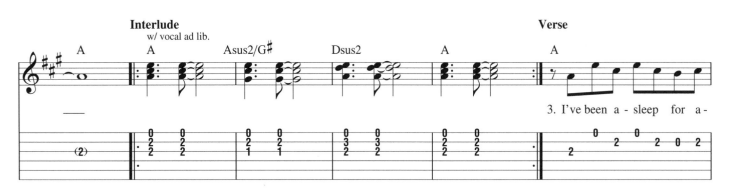

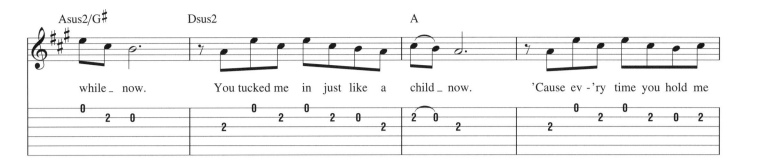

while _ now. You tucked me in just like a child _ now. 'Cause ev-'ry time you hold me

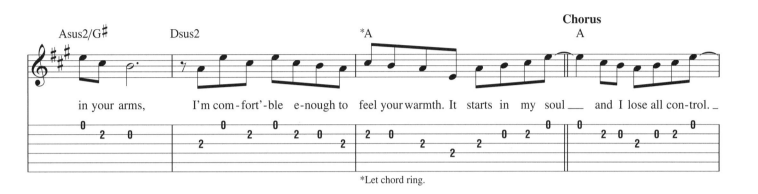

Chorus

in your arms, I'm com-fort'-ble e-nough to feel your warmth. It starts in my soul __ and I lose all con-trol. _

*Let chord ring.

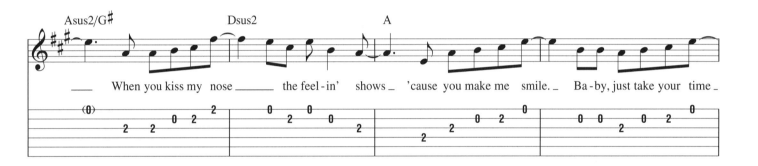

__ When you kiss my nose _____ the feel-in' shows _ 'cause you make me smile. Ba-by, just take your time _

Outro
Slower

__ now, hold-in' me tight _____ Wher-ev-er, _____ where-ev-er, _____ wher-

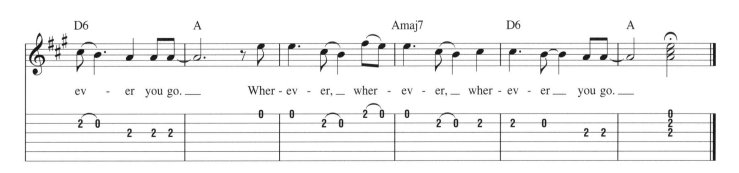

ev - er you go. __ Wher-ev-er, __ wher-ev-er, __ wher-ev-er __ you go. __

Black Horse and the Cherry Tree

Words and Music by Katie Tunstall

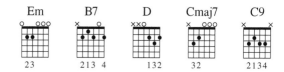

Strum Pattern: 2, 3
Pick Pattern: 3, 4

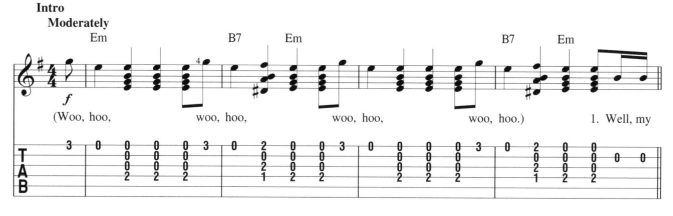

big black horse and a cher - ry tree. (Woo, hoo, woo, hoo.) I

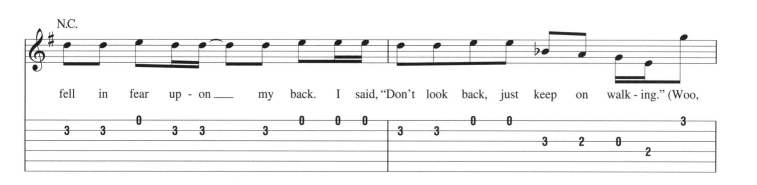

fell in fear up - on ____ my back. I said, "Don't look back, just keep on walk - ing." (Woo,

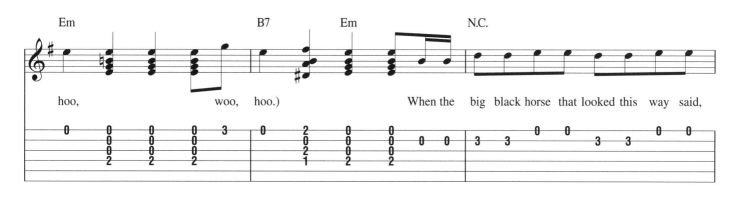

hoo, woo, hoo.) When the big black horse that looked this way said,

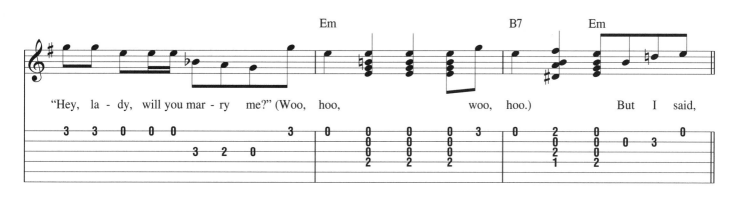

"Hey, la - dy, will you mar - ry me?" (Woo, hoo, woo, hoo.) But I said,

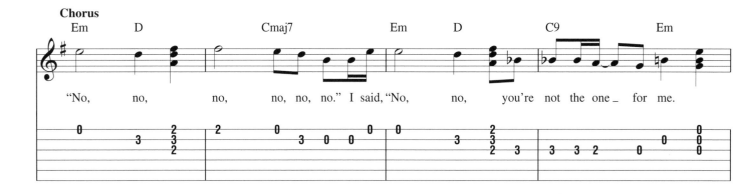

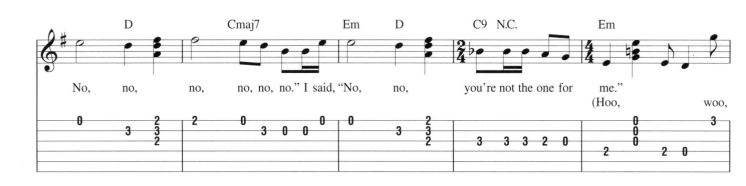

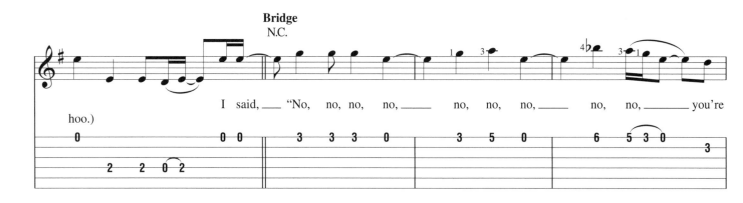

not the one __ for me. No, no, no, no, no, no, no,
(Woo, hoo, woo, hoo, woo,

Outro-Chorus

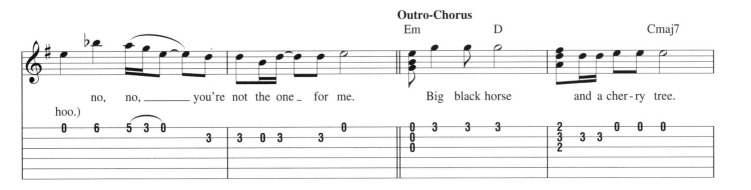

Em   D   Cmaj7

no, no, __ you're not the one _ for me. Big black horse and a cher-ry tree.
hoo.)

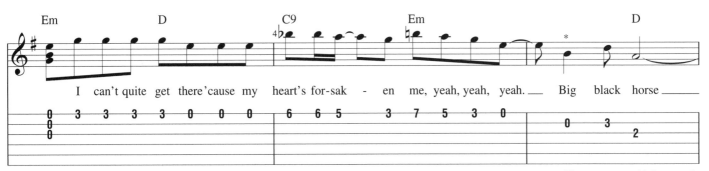

Em   D   C9   Em   D

I can't quite get there 'cause my heart's for-sak - en me, yeah, yeah, yeah. __ Big black horse __

*Sung one octave higher to end.

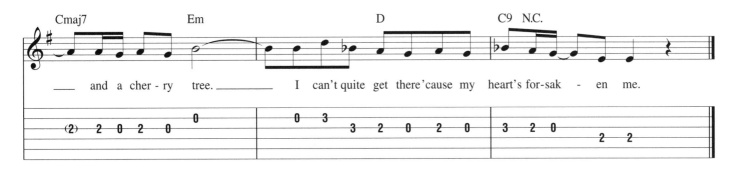

Cmaj7   Em   D   C9 N.C.

__ and a cher-ry tree. __ I can't quite get there 'cause my heart's for-sak - en me.

Additional Lyrics

2. And my heart had a problem in the early hours
   So I stopped it dead for a beat or two. (Woo, hoo, woo, hoo.)
   But I cut some cord and I shouldn't have done that,
   And it won't forgive me after all these years. (Woo, hoo, woo, hoo.)
   So I sent it to a place in the middle of nowhere
   With a big black horse and a cherry tree. (Woo, hoo, woo, hoo.)
   Now, it won't come back 'cause it's oh, so happy
   And now I got a hole for the world to see. (Woo, hoo, woo, hoo.)
   And it said,...

Detroit Rock City

Words and Music by Paul Stanley and Bob Ezrin

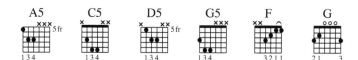

Strum Pattern: 1
Pick Pattern: 1

Intro

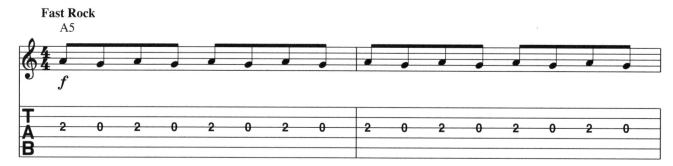

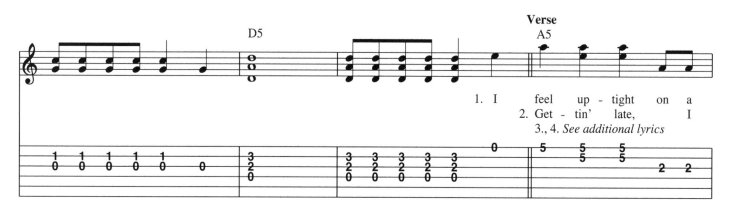

1. I feel up-tight on a
2. Get-tin' late, I
3., 4. *See additional lyrics*

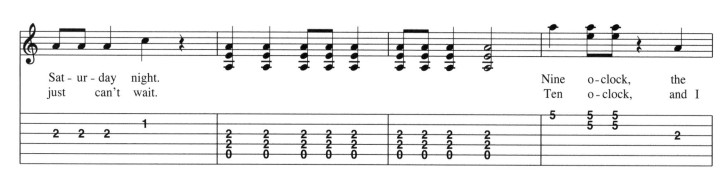

Sat-ur-day night.   Nine o-clock,   the
just can't wait.   Ten o-clock, and I

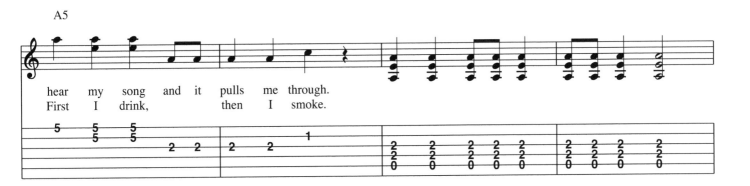

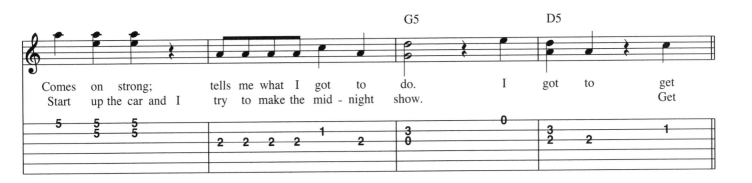

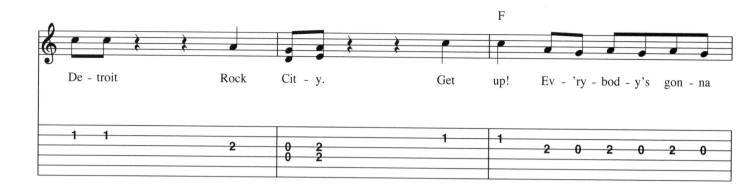

De - troit   Rock   Cit - y.   Get   up!   Ev - 'ry - bod - y's   gon - na

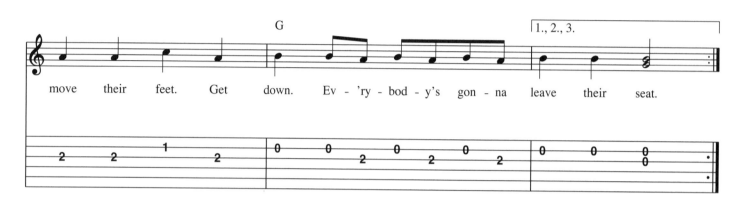

move   their   feet.   Get   down.   Ev - 'ry - bod - y's   gon - na   leave   their   seat.

Get   up!   Ev - 'ry - bod - y's   gon - na

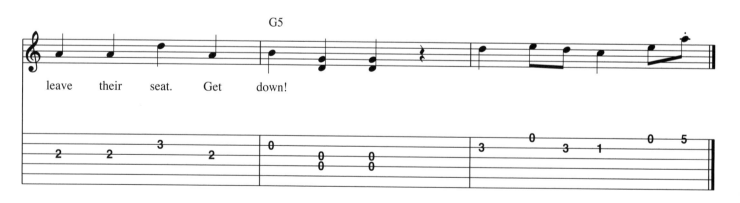

leave   their   seat.   Get   down!

Additional Lyrics

3. Movin' fast doin' ninety five.
   Hit top speed, but I'm still movin' much too slow.
   Feel so good; I'm so alive.
   Hear my song, playin' on the radio. It goes;

4. Twelve o'clock, I gotta rock.
   There's a truck ahead, lights starin' at my eyes.
   Whoa, my God, no time to turn,
   I got to laugh, 'cause I know I'm gonna die. Why?

Don't Bring Me Down

Words and Music by Jeff Lynne

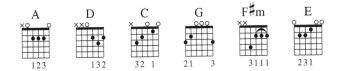

Strum Pattern: 1
Pick Pattern: 1

Intro
Moderately

1. You got me run-ning, go-ing out of my mind._ You got me think-ing that I'm

2., 3., 4., 6. *See additional lyrics*

wast-ing my time._ Don't bring me down. No, no, no, no, no._ Oo,_ hoo._ I'll

tell you once more _ be-fore I get off the floor. Don't bring me down. _____ down.

Chorus

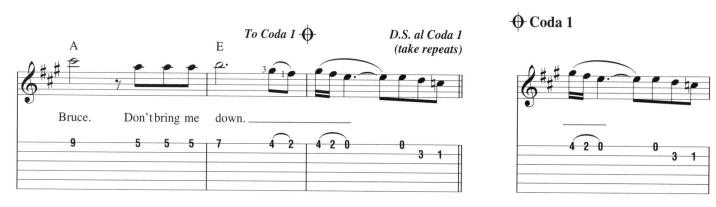

Don't bring me down, _ Bruce. Don't bring me down, _ Bruce. Don't bring me down, _

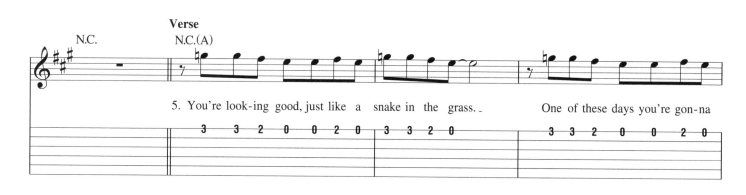

Bruce. Don't bring me down. _____

Coda 1

Verse

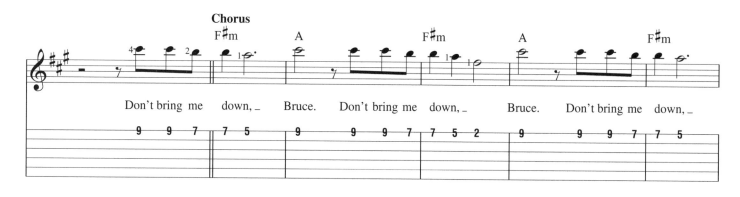

5. You're look-ing good, just like a snake in the grass. _ One of these days you're gon-na

break your glass. _ Don't bring me down. No, no, no, no, no, no, no, no, no. Oo, _ hoo. _ I'll

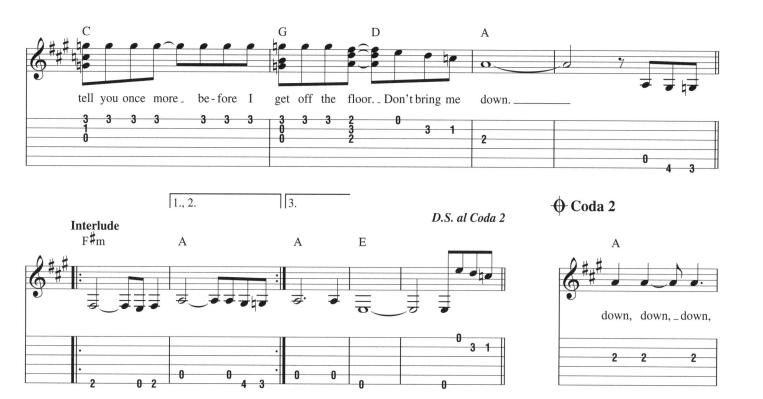

tell you once more before I get off the floor. Don't bring me down.

[1., 2.]   [3.]

D.S. al Coda 2

⊕ **Coda 2**

Interlude

down, down, down,

Outro

down, down, down.

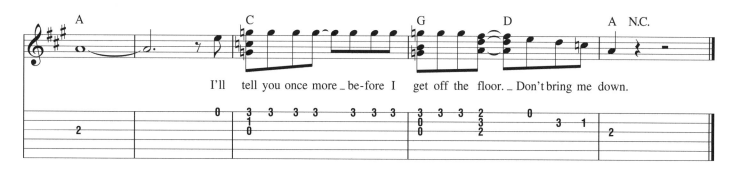

I'll tell you once more before I get off the floor. Don't bring me down.

Additional Lyrics

2. You wanna stay out with your fancy friends.
I'm telling you, it's gotta be the end.
Don't bring me down. No, no, no, no, no. Oo, hoo.
I'll tell you once more before I get off the floor.
Don't bring me down.

3. What happened to the girl I use to know?
You let your mind out somewhere down the road.
Don't bring me down. No, no, no, no, no. Oo, hoo.
I'll tell you once more before I get off the floor.
Don't bring me down.

4. You're always talking 'bout your crazy nights.
One of these days, you're gonna get it right.
Don't bring me down. No, no, no, no, no. Oo, hoo.
I'll tell you once more before I get off the floor.
Don't bring me down.

6. You got me shaking, got me running away.
You got me crawling up to you every day.
Don't bring me down. No, no, no, no, no. Oo, hoo.
I'll tell you once more before I get off the floor.
Don't bring me down.

Heart Full of Soul

Words and Music by Graham Gouldman

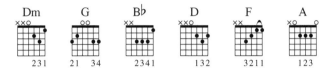

Strum Pattern: 4, 6
Pick Pattern: 4, 5

Intro

Moderately

Play 4 times

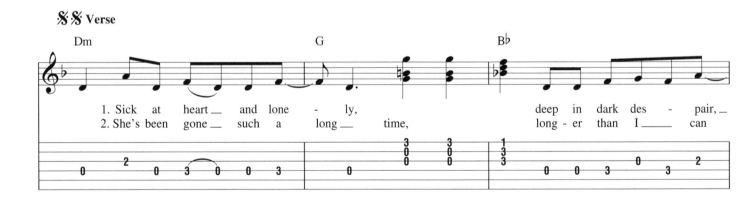

1. Sick at heart and lone-ly,   deep in dark des - pair,
2. She's been gone such a long time,   long - er than I can

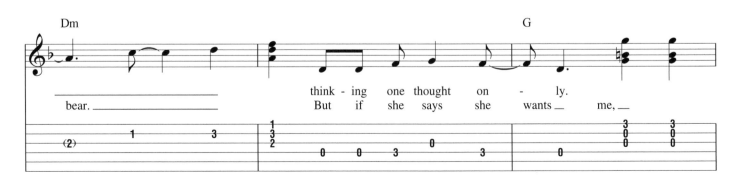

bear.   think - ing one thought on - ly.
    But if she says she wants me,

Where is she,___ tell me where?
tell her that I'll be there.

And if she says

to you she don't___ love___ me,_____

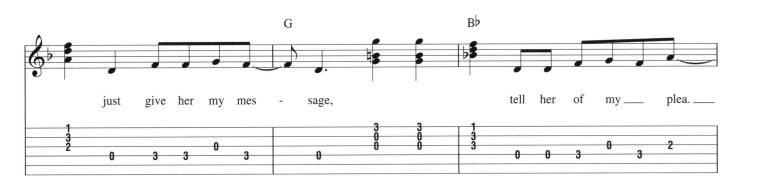

just give her my mes - sage, tell her of my___ plea.___

𝄋 **Chorus**

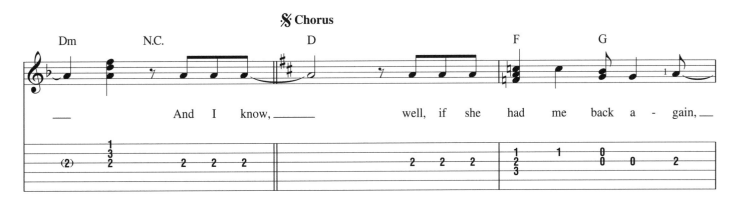

And I know,_____ well, if she had me back a - gain,___

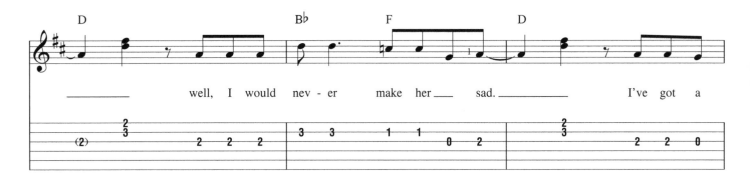

well, I would nev - er make her ___ sad. _____ I've got a

To Coda 1 ⊕
To Coda 2 ⊕
Interlude

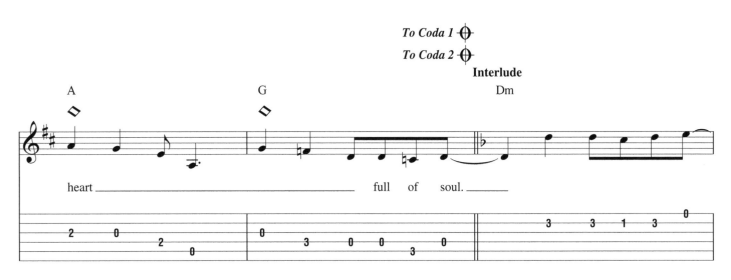

heart _____ full of soul. _____

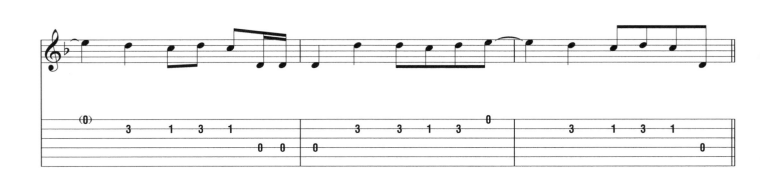

Guitar Solo

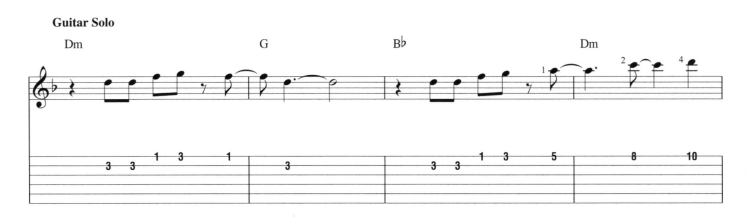

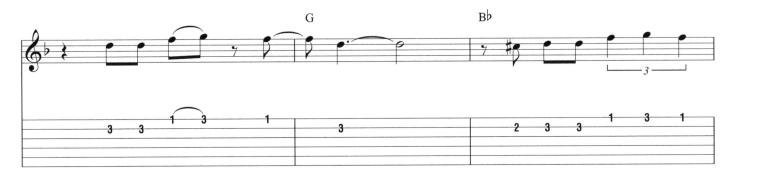

G   B♭

Coda 1

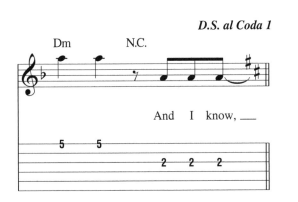

Dm   N.C.

And I know, ___

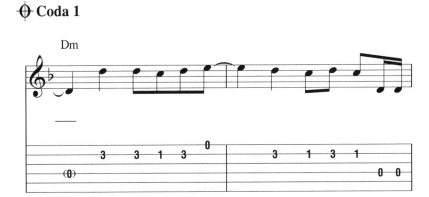

Dm

___

Coda 2

D.S.S. al Coda 2

D.S. al Coda 1

Outro

Dm

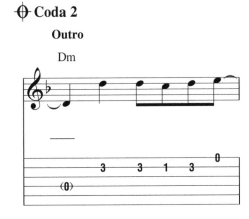

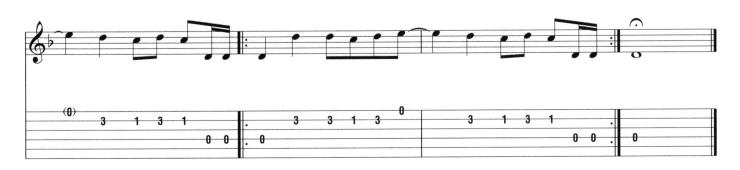

I Kissed a Girl

Words and Music by Cathy Dennis, Max Martin, Lukasz Gottwald and Katy Perry

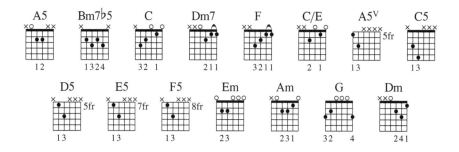

Strum Pattern: 3, 4
Pick Pattern: 1, 6

Verse

1. This was nev-er the way __ I planned, not my in-ten-tion. I got so
2. No, I don't e-ven know __ your name. It does-n't mat-ter. You're my ex-

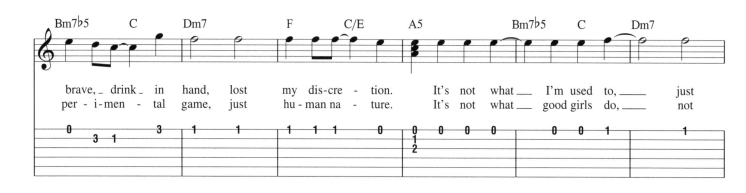

brave, __ drink in hand, lost my dis-cre-tion. It's not what __ I'm used to, __ just
per-i-men-tal game, just hu-man na-ture. It's not what __ good girls do, __ not

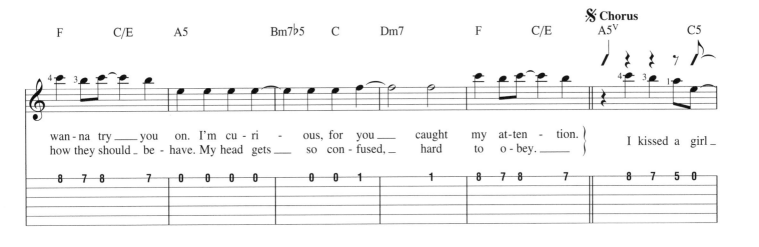

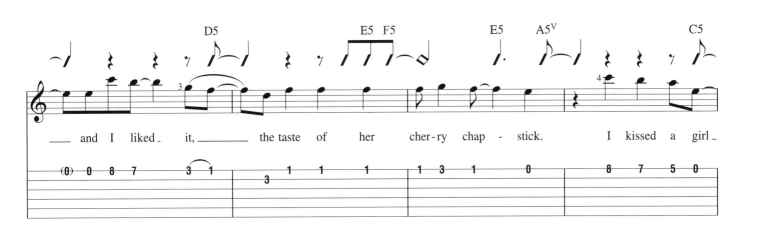

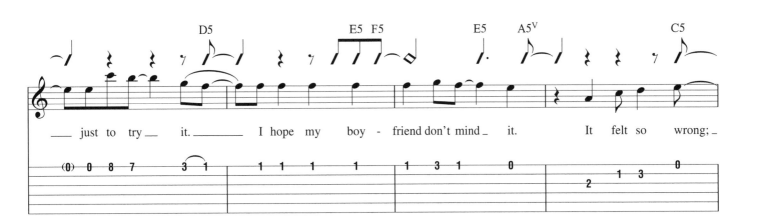

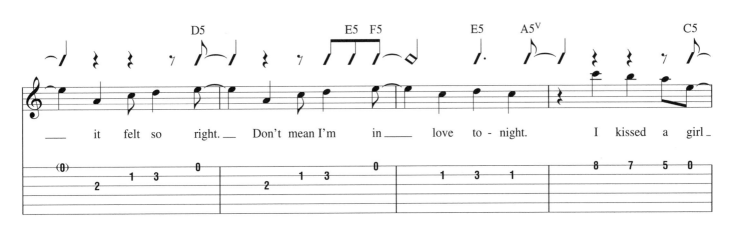

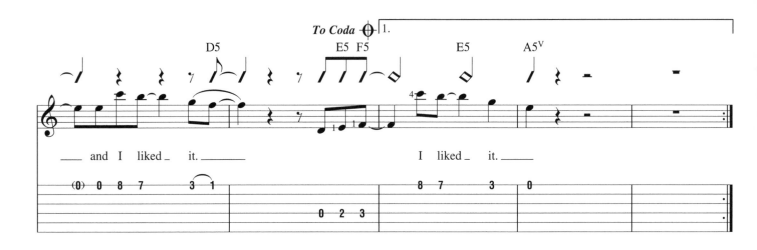

and I liked _ it. _____   I liked _ it. _____

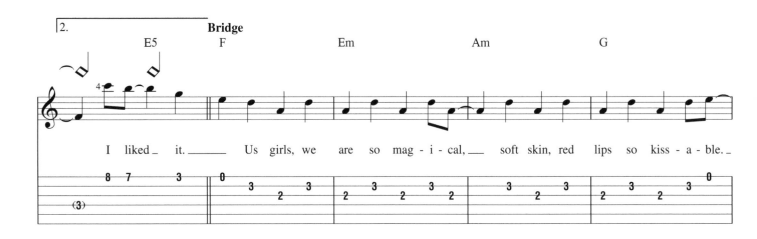

I liked _ it. _____ Us girls, we are so mag - i - cal, ___ soft skin, red lips so kiss - a - ble. _

___ Hard to re - sist, so touch - a - ble. _ And too good _ to de - ny _ it. ___ Ain't no big

*Sung one octave higher to end of Bridge.

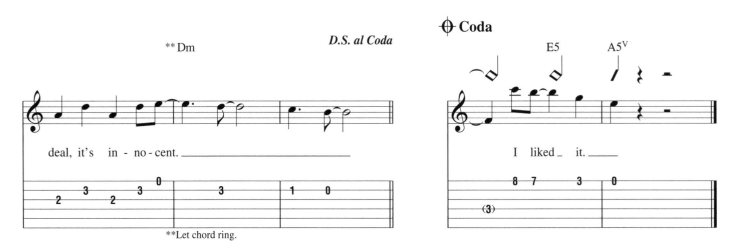

deal, it's in - no - cent. _____   I liked _ it. _____

**Let chord ring.

Pork and Beans

Words and Music by Rivers Cuomo

*Tune down 1/2 step:
(low to high) E♭-A♭-D♭-G♭-B♭-E♭

Strum Pattern: 1, 4
Pick Pattern: 4, 5

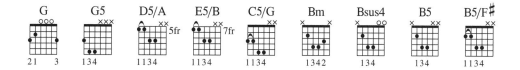

*Optional: To match recording, tune down 1/2 step.

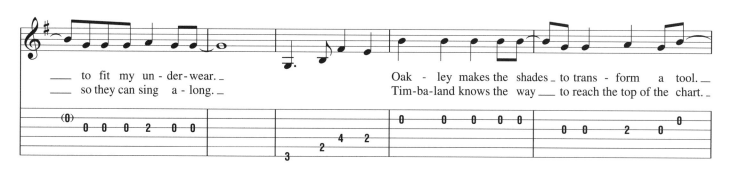

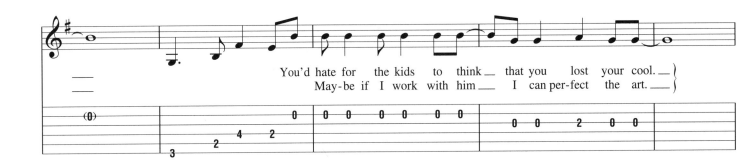

You'd hate for the kids to think __ that you lost your cool. __
May-be if I work with him __ I can per-fect the art. __

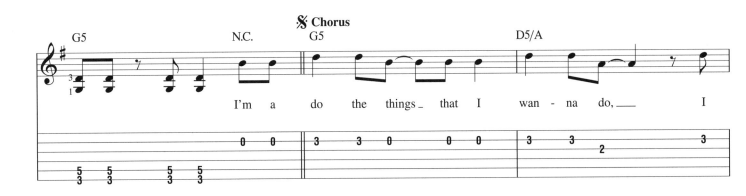

%. **Chorus**

G5   N.C.   G5   D5/A

I'm a do the things __ that I wan - na do, __ I

E5/B   C5/G   G5   D5/A

ain't got a thing to prove to you. __ I'll eat my can - dy with the pork and beans, ex -

E5/B   C5/G   G5   D5/A

cuse my man - ners if I make a scene. I ain't gon - na wear the clothes __ that you like. I'm

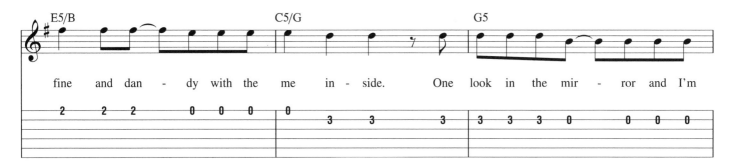

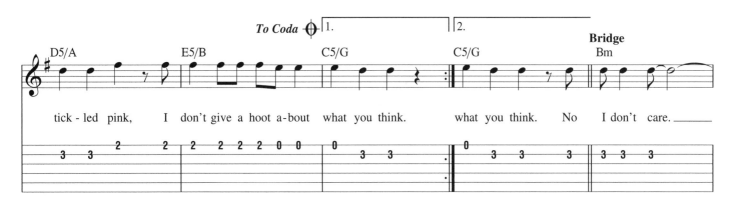

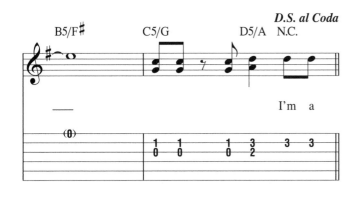
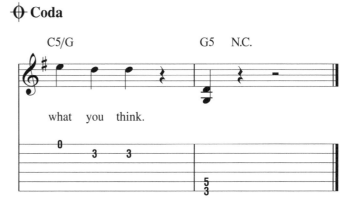

I'm So Sick

Words and Music by Sameer Bhattacharya, Jared Hartmann, Kirkpatrick Seals, James Culpepper and Lacey Mosley

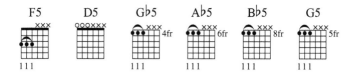

*Drop D tuning:
(low to high) D-A-D-G-B-E

Strum Pattern: 3
Pick Pattern: 3

Intro
Moderate Rock

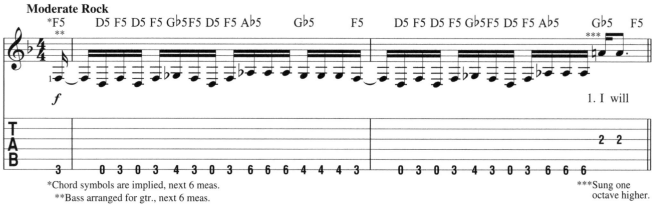

*Chord symbols are implied, next 6 meas.
**Bass arranged for gtr., next 6 meas.

***Sung one octave higher.

†Gtr. enters.

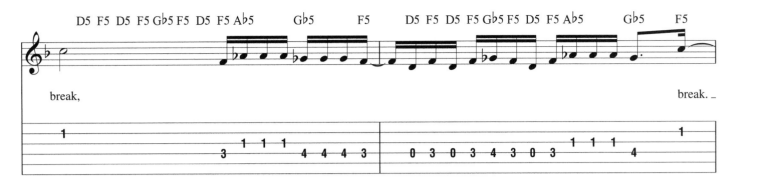

break,   break.

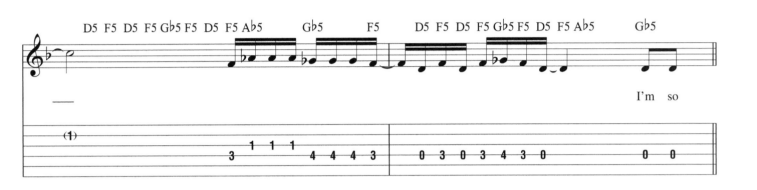

___   I'm so

Chorus

sick, in-fect-ed with where I live. Let me live with-out __ this emp-ty bliss, self-ish-ness. __ I'm so sick. __

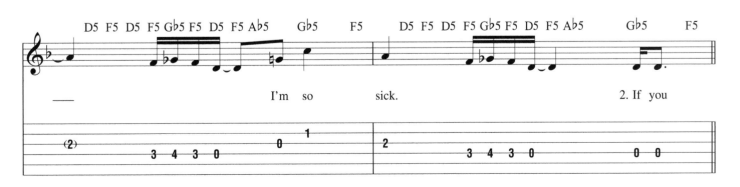

___   I'm so   sick.   2. If you

85

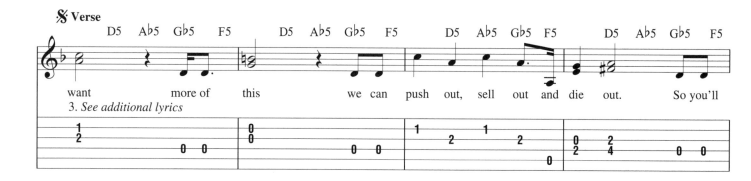

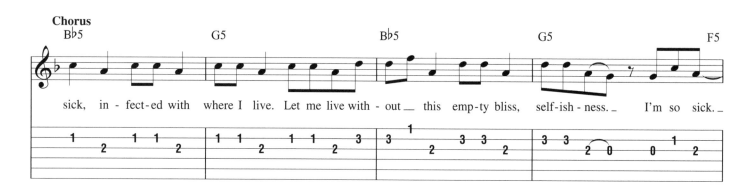

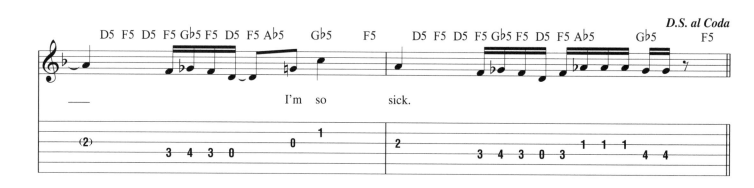

Chorus

sick, in - fect-ed with where I live. Let me live with - out __ this emp-ty bliss, self-ish - ness. __ I'm so, __

I'm so sick. I'm so

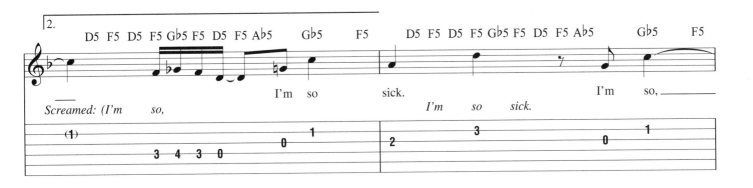

Screamed: (I'm so, I'm so sick. I'm so, _____

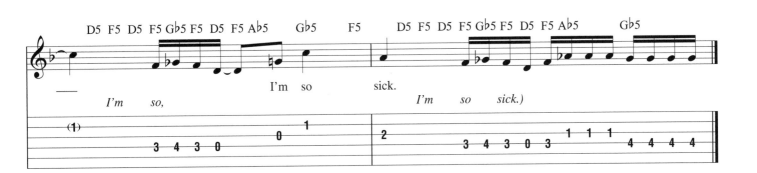

I'm so, I'm so sick. I'm so sick.)

Additional Lyrics

2. Hear it. I'm screaming it.
   You're heading to it now.
   Hear it. I'm screaming it.
   You tremble at this sound.

Long Time

Words and Music by Tom Scholz

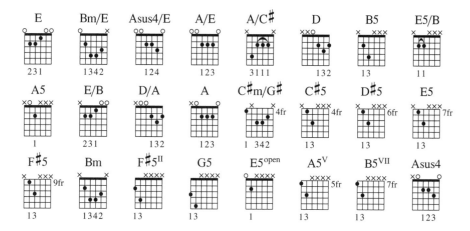

*Capo I

Strum Pattern: 5
Pick Pattern: 3

1. It's been such a long time, ___

2., 3. *See additional lyrics*

*Optional: To match recording, place capo at first fret.

I think I should be go - in', yeah. And time does-n't wait for me, _

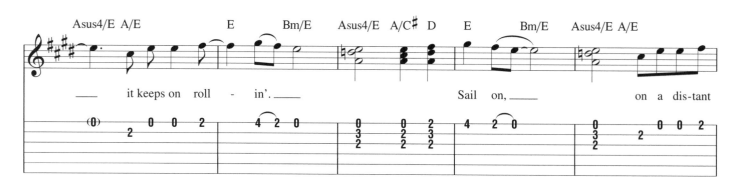

___ it keeps on roll - in'. ___ Sail on, ___ on a dis-tant

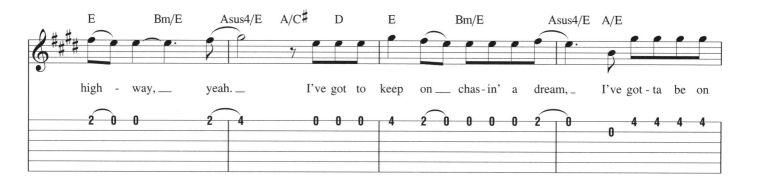

high - way, __ yeah. __ I've got to keep on __ chas-in' a dream, _ I've got-ta be on

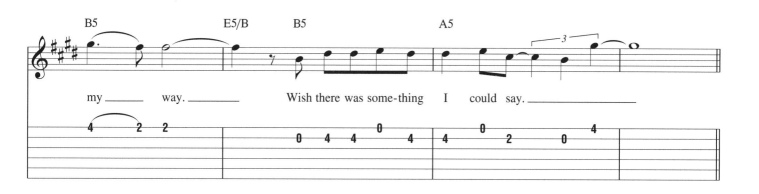

my ____ way. __ Wish there was some-thing I could say. _____

Interlude

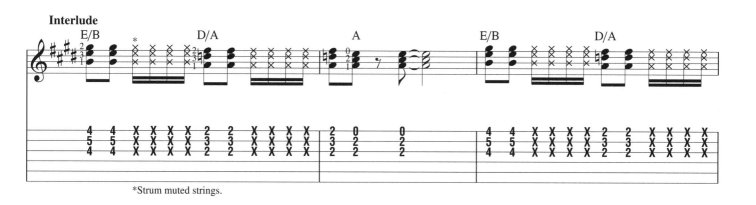

*Strum muted strings.

To Coda 2 ⊕

Chorus

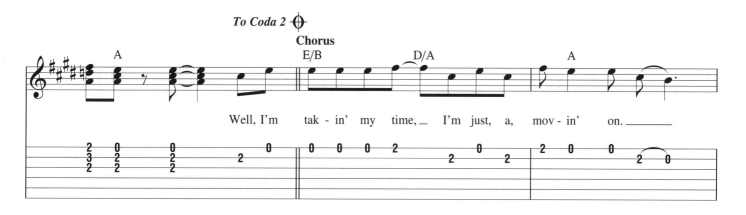

Well, I'm tak-in' my time, _ I'm just, a, mov-in' on. _____

You'll for - get a - bout me af - ter I've been gone. _ And I take what I find. _ I don't _

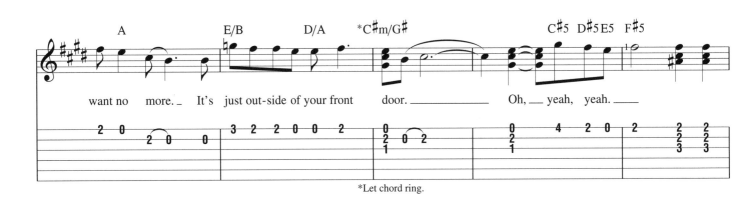

want no more. _ It's just out-side of your front door. _____ Oh, _ yeah, yeah. _

*Let chord ring.

To Coda 1 ⊕

Guitar Solo

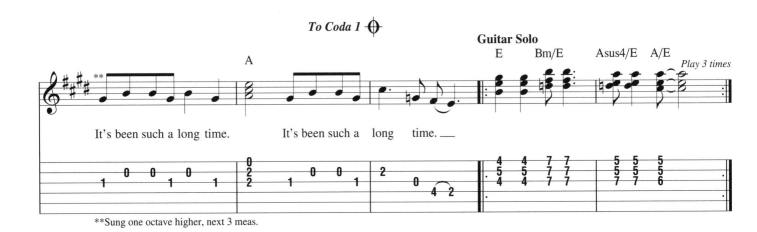

It's been such a long time. It's been such a long time. _

**Sung one octave higher, next 3 meas.

⊕ **Coda 1**

D.S. al Coda 1

2. Well, _ I get

Guitar Solo

long time. _____

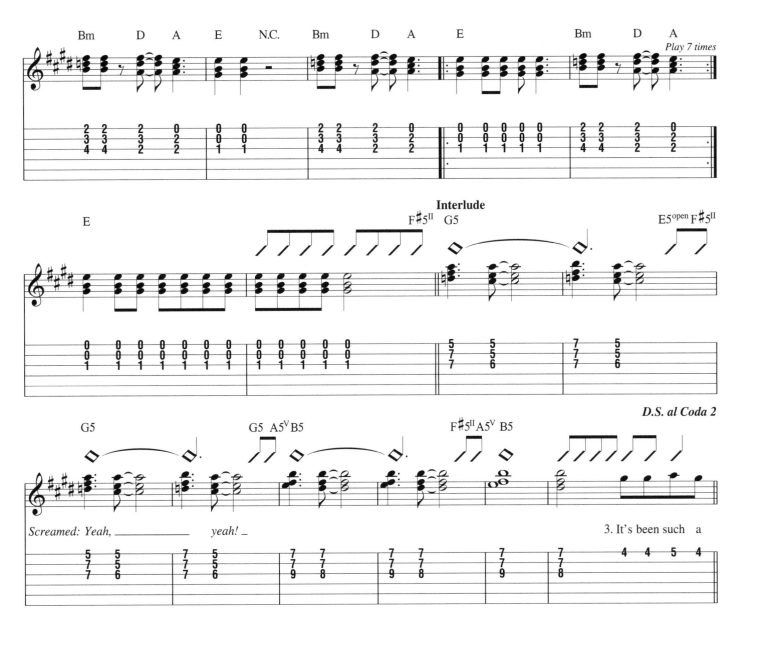

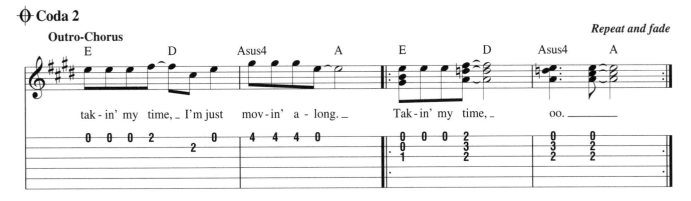

Additional Lyrics

2. Well, I get so lonely when I am without you.
   But in my mind, deep in my mind, I can't forget about you, whoa.
   Good times, and faces that remind me, yeah.
   I'm tryin' to forget your name and leave it all behind me.
   You're comin' back to find me.

3. It's been such a long time, I think I should be goin', yeah.
   And time doesn't wait for me, it keeps on rollin'.
   There's a long road I gotta stay in time with, yeah.
   I've got to keep on chasin' that dream, though I may never find it.
   I'm always just behind it.

Makes Me Wonder

Words by Adam Levine
Music by Adam Levine, Jesse Carmichael and Mickey Madden

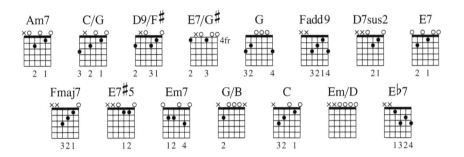

*Capo II
Strum Pattern: 1, 2
Pick Pattern: 2, 5

Intro
Moderately

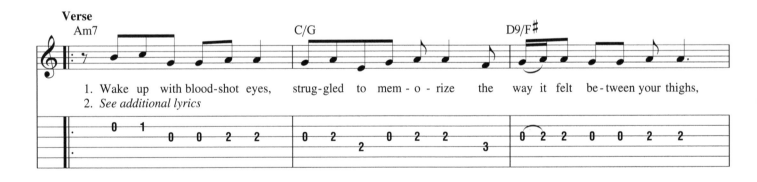

*Optional: To match recording, place capo at 2nd fret.

1. Wake up with blood-shot eyes, strug-gled to mem-o-rize the way it felt be-tween your thighs,
2. *See additional lyrics*

pleas-ure that made you cry. Uh, feels so good to be bad, not worth the af-ter-math. Af-

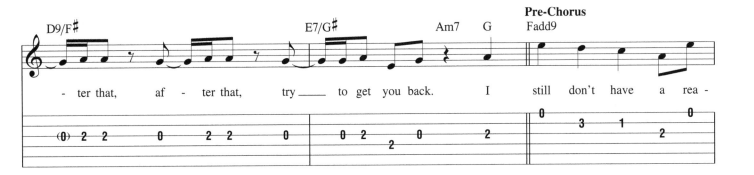

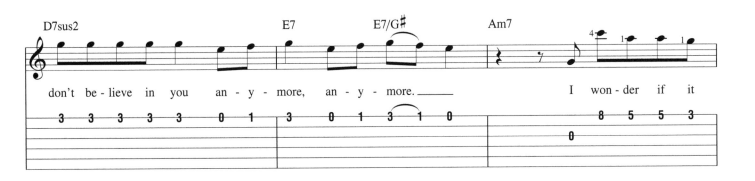

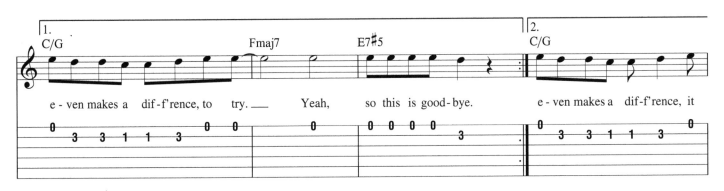

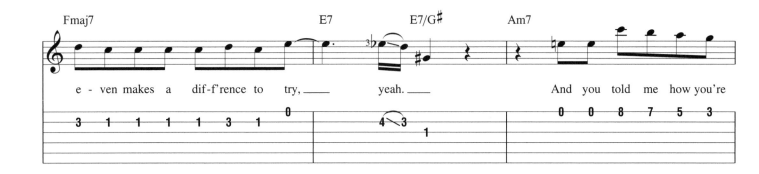

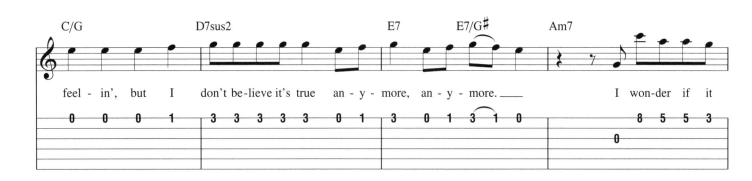

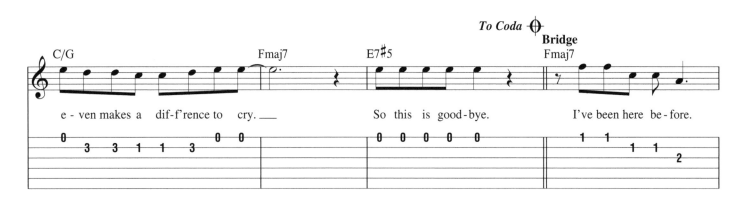

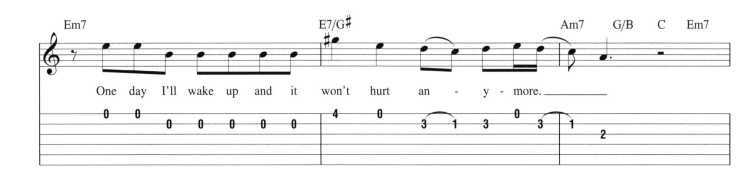

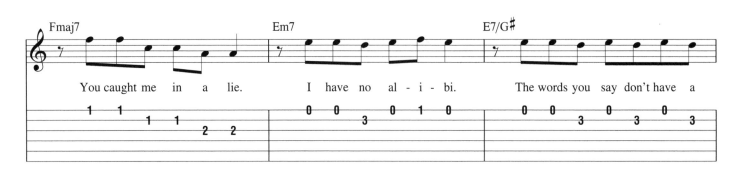

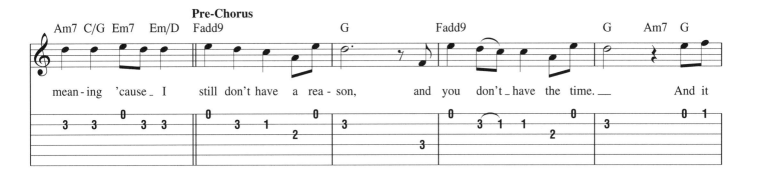

Pre-Chorus

mean - ing 'cause _ I still don't have a rea - son, and you don't _ have the time. _ And it

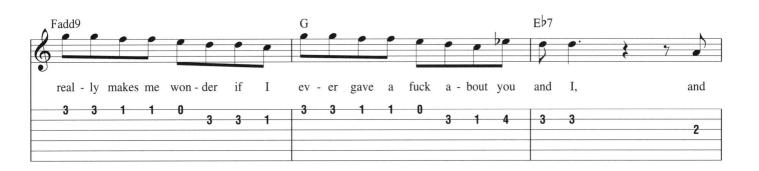

real - ly makes me won - der if I ev - er gave a fuck a - bout you and I, and

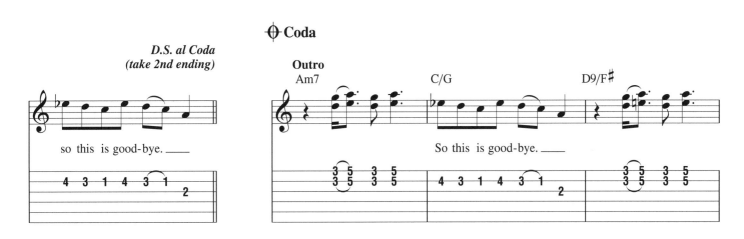

Coda

D.S. al Coda
(take 2nd ending)

Outro

so this is good-bye. _ So this is good-bye. _

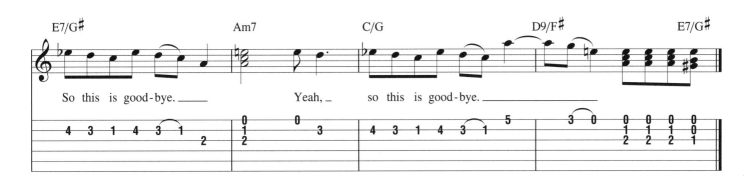

So this is good-bye. _ Yeah, _ so this is good-bye. _

Additional Lyrics

2. Goddamn, my spinnin' head, decisions that make my bed.
Now I must lay in it and deal with things I've left unsaid.
I want to dive into you, forget what you're goin' through.
I get behind; make your move. Forget about the truth.

Mrs. Robinson

from THE GRADUATE

Words and Music by Paul Simon

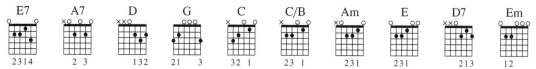

*Capo II

Strum Pattern: 3, 5
Pick Pattern: 1, 3

Intro
  Moderately fast

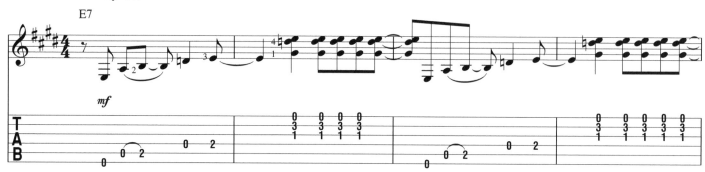

*Optional: To match recording, place capo at 2nd fret.

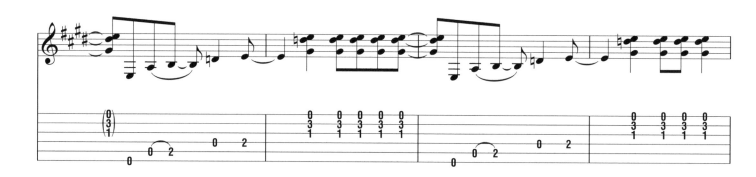

Dee, dee, dee, dee, dee, dee, dee, dee, dee, dee, dee, dee, dee.____

Doo, doo, doo, doo, doo, doo, doo, doo, doo.____

Dee, dee, dee, dee, dee, dee, dee, dee, dee, __ dee, dee, dee, dee. __

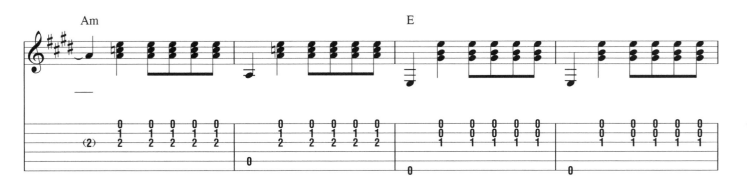

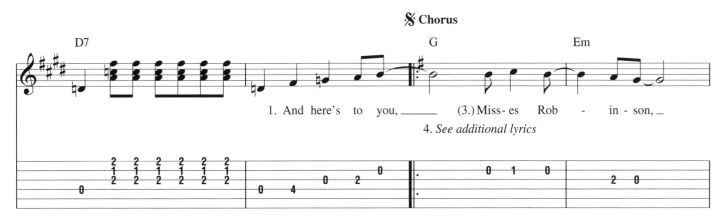

𝄋 Chorus

1. And here's to you, ____ (3.) Miss- es Rob - in - son, __

4. *See additional lyrics*

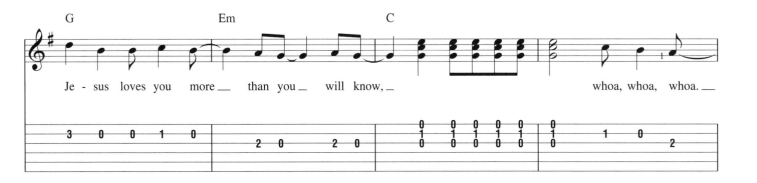

Je - sus loves you more __ than you __ will know, __ whoa, whoa, whoa. __

__ God bless you please, __ Miss- es Ro - bin - son. __

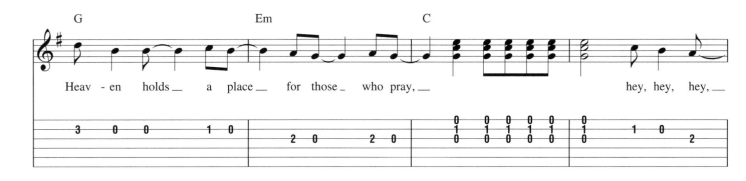

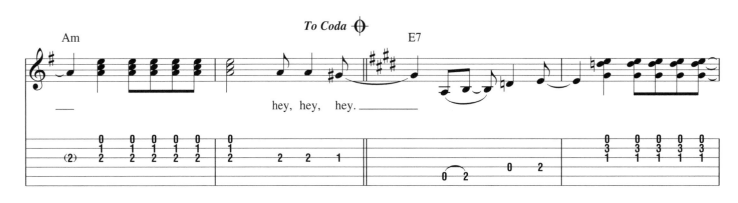

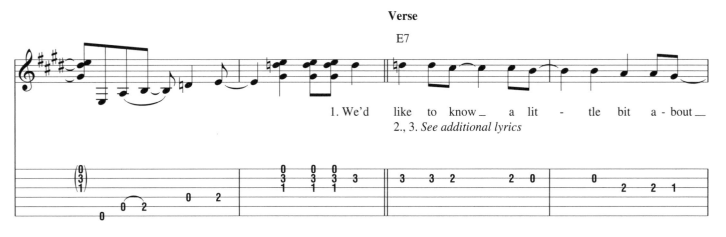

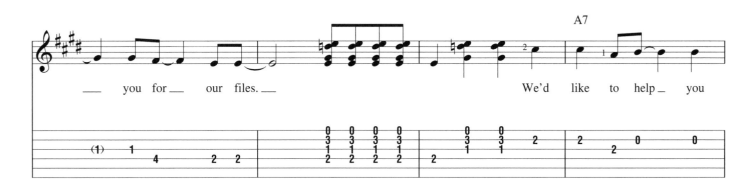

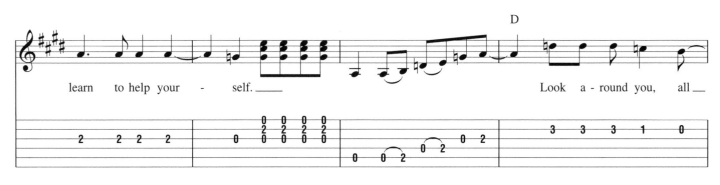

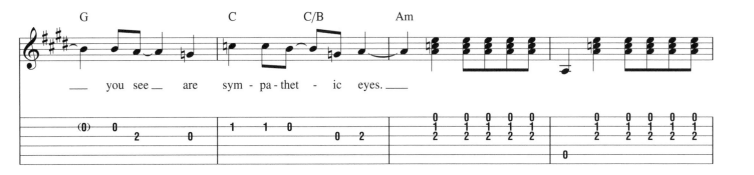

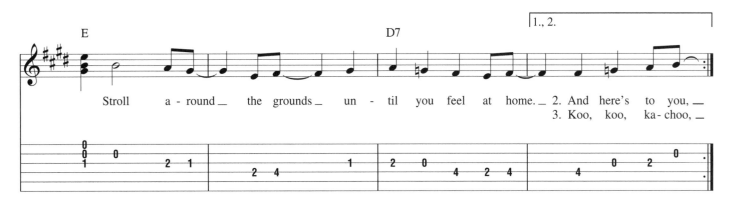

you see __ are sym - pa - thet - ic eyes. __

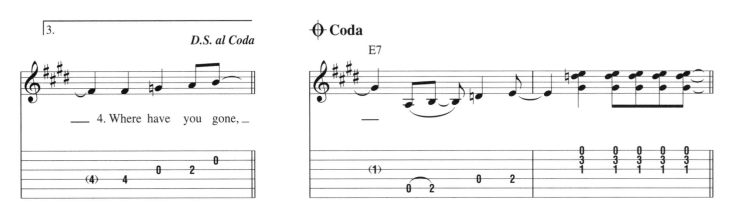

Stroll a - round __ the grounds __ un - til you feel at home. __ 2. And here's to you, __
3. Koo, koo, ka - choo, __

3.

D.S. al Coda

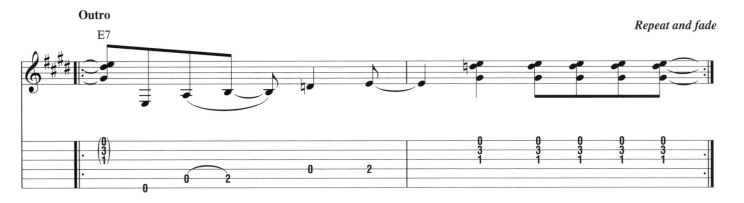

__ 4. Where have you gone, __

⊕ Coda

__

Outro

Repeat and fade

Additional Lyrics

2. Hide it in a hiding place where no one ever goes.
Put in in your pantry with your cupcakes.
It's a little secret, just the Robinsons' affair.
Most of all you've got to hide it from the kids.

3. Sitting on a sofa on a Sunday afternoon.
Going to the candidates debate.
Laugh about it, shout about it when you've got to choose.
Ev'ry way you look at this you lose.

Chorus 4. Where have you gone, Joe DiMaggio?
A nation turns its lonely eyes to you, woo, woo, woo.
What's that you say, Mrs. Robinson?
Joltin' Joe has left and gone away,
Hey, hey, hey, hey, hey, hey.

Panama

Words and Music by David Lee Roth, Edward Van Halen, Alex Van Halen and Michael Anthony

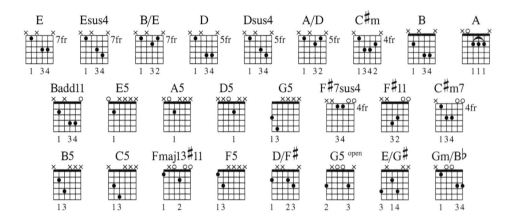

*Tune down 1/2 step:
(low to high) E♭-A♭-D♭-G♭-B♭-E♭

Strum Pattern: 1, 4
Pick Pattern: 2, 4
Intro
Moderate Rock

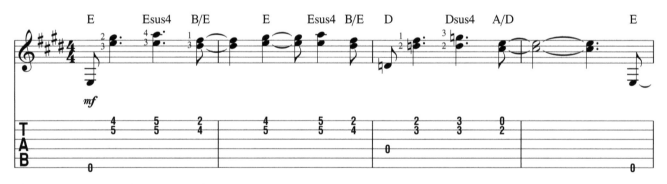

*Optional: To match recording, tune down 1/2 step.

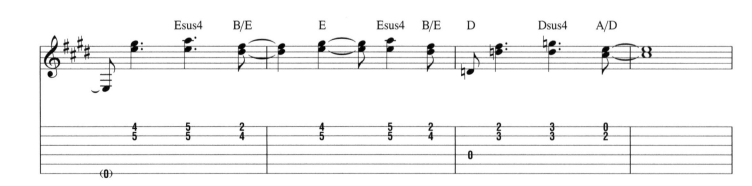

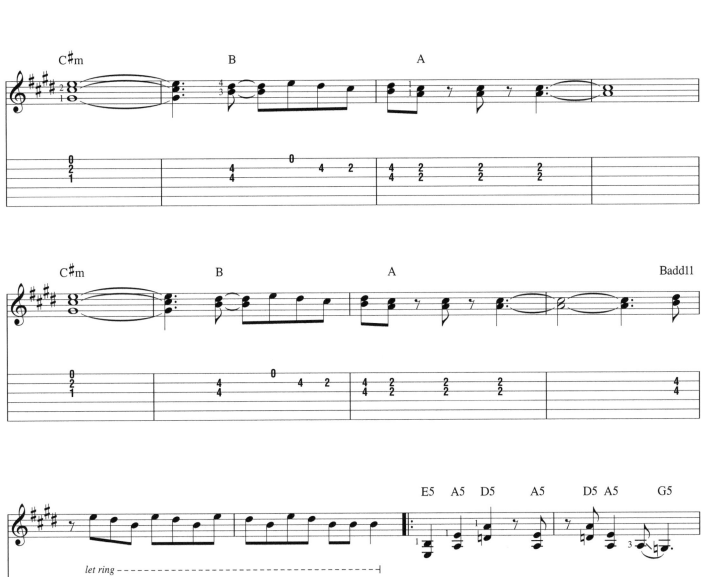

Verse

1. Jump back. What's that sound? __
2. *See additional lyrics*

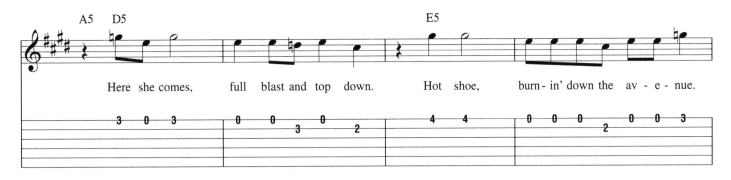

Here she comes, full blast and top down. Hot shoe, burn-in' down the av - e - nue.

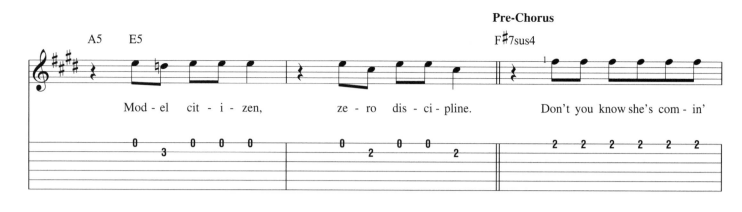

Mod - el cit - i - zen, ze - ro dis - ci - pline. Don't you know she's com - in'

home __ to me? _____ You'll lose her in the turn. __ *Spoken: I'll get her.*

*Lyrics in italics are spoken throughout.

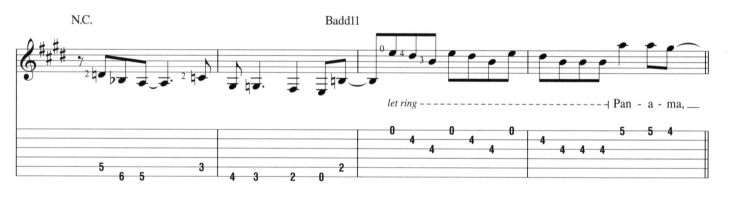

let ring - Pan - a - ma, __

Chorus

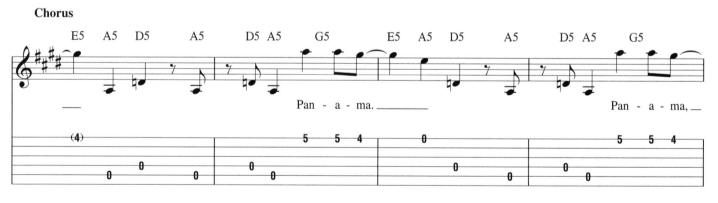

__ Pan - a - ma. _____ Pan - a - ma,

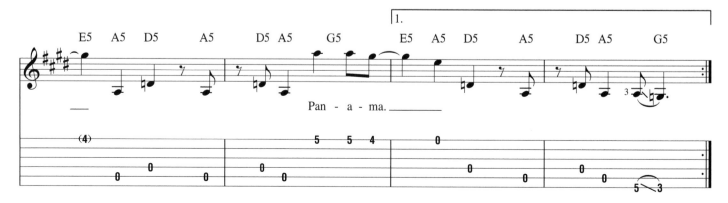

__ Pan - a - ma. _____

Yeah, we're run-nin' a lit-tle bit hot to-night.

I can bare - ly see the road from the heat com - in' off it.

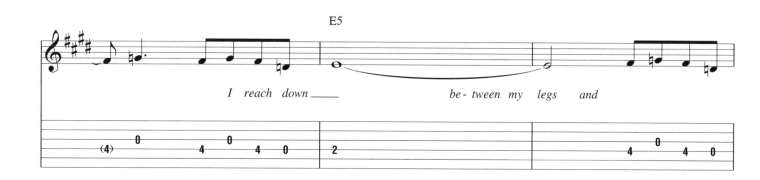

I reach down _____ be - tween my legs and

ease the seat _____ back. She's blind - in',

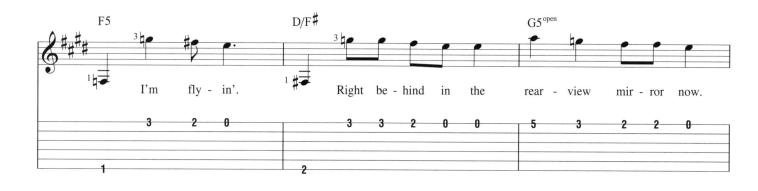

I'm fly - in'. Right be - hind in the rear - view mir - ror now.

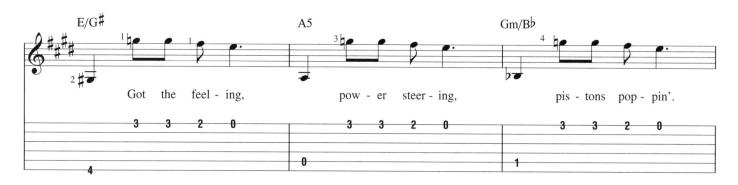

Got the feel - ing, pow - er steer - ing, pis - tons pop - pin'.

Chorus

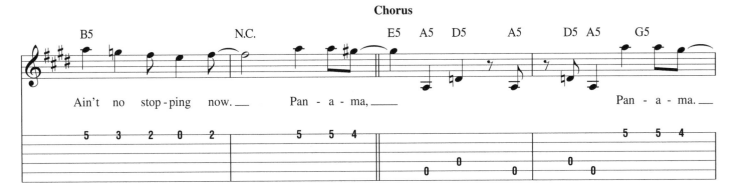

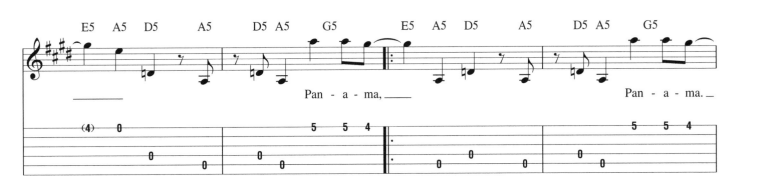

Additional Lyrics

2. Ain't nothin' like it, her shiny machine,
   Got the feel for the wheel, keep the moving parts clean.
   Hot shoe, burnin' down the avenue,
   Got an on-ramp comin' through my bedroom.

Rehab

Words and Music by Amy Winehouse

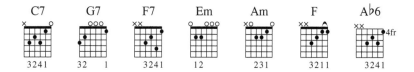

Strum Pattern: 6
Pick Pattern: 4

Chorus
Moderately

They tried to make me go to re-hab, I said, "No, no, no."

Yes, I been black, but when I come back, you won't know, know, know.

I ain't got the time, and if my dad-dy thinks I'm

fine, _ he's tried to make me go to re - hab, _ I _ won't _ go, _ go, _ go. _

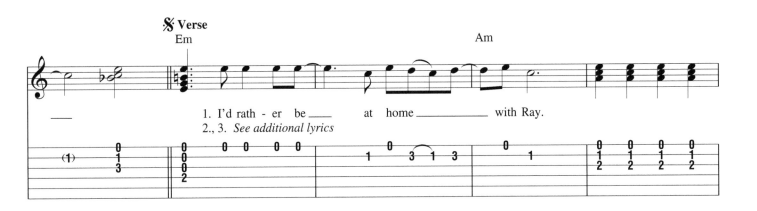

§ **Verse**

1. I'd rath - er be _ at home _ with Ray.
2., 3. *See additional lyrics*

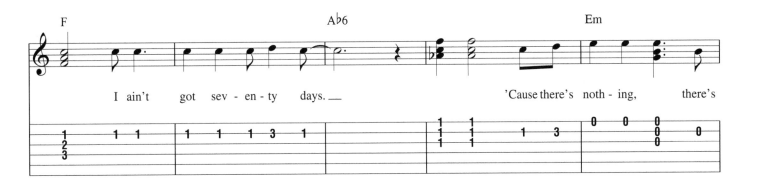

I ain't got sev - en - ty days. _ 'Cause there's noth - ing, there's

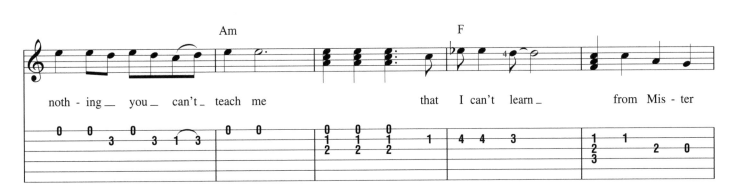

noth - ing _ you _ can't _ teach me that I can't learn _ from Mis - ter

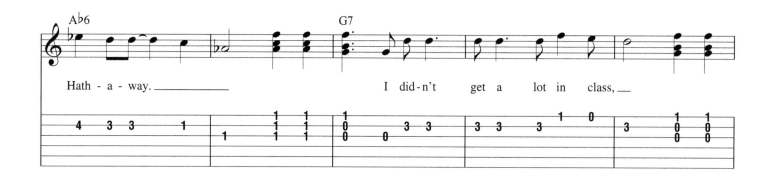

Hath - a - way. _____ I did-n't get a lot in class, __

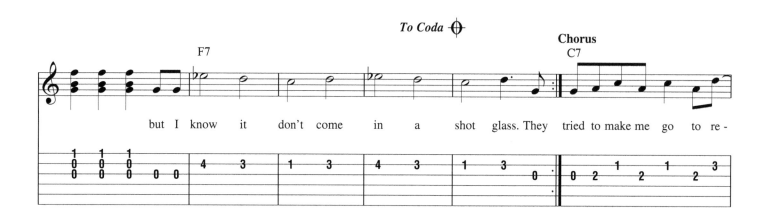

but I know it don't come in a shot glass. They tried to make me go to re-

- hab, _ I ___ said, __ "No, _____ no, ____ no." __ Yes, ___ I been _ black, but when _

__ I come _ back, you won't know, __ know, _ know. _

dried. _____ They

Outro-Chorus

tried to make me go to re - hab, I _ said, _ "No, _ no, _ no." _ Yes, _

_ I been _ black, but when _ I come _ back, you won't know, _ know, _ know. _

I ain't got the time, _ and if my dad - dy _ thinks _ I'm _ fine, _ he's

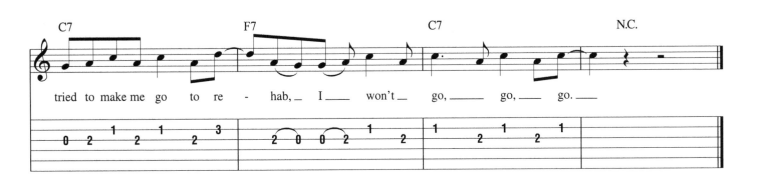

tried to make me go to re - hab, I _ won't _ go, _ go, _ go.

Additional Lyrics

2. The man said, "Why you think you're here?"
   I said, "I got no idea."
   I'm gonna, I'm gonna lose my baby,
   So I always keep a bottle near."
   Said, "I just think you're depressed,
   Kiss me, baby, and go rest."

3. I won't ever want to drink again.
   I just, ooh, I just need a friend.
   I'm not gonna spend ten weeks,
   Have everyone think I'm on the mend.
   It's not just my pride,
   It's just 'til these tears have dried.

Teardrops on My Guitar

Words and Music by Taylor Swift and Liz Rose

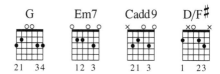

*Capo III

Strum Pattern: 3, 6
Pick Pattern: 2, 5

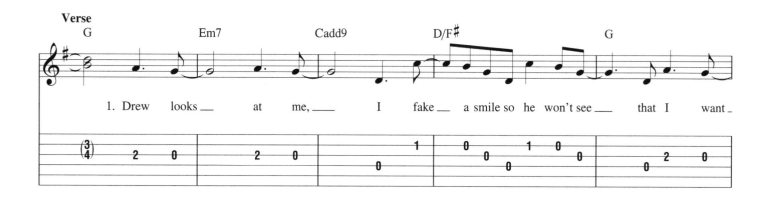

*Optional: To match recording, place capo at 3rd fret.

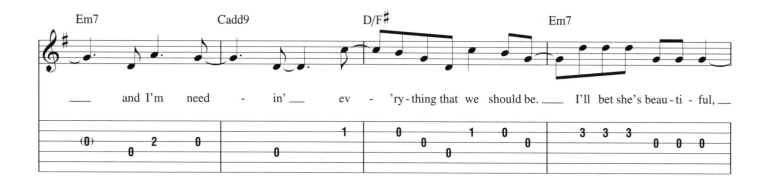

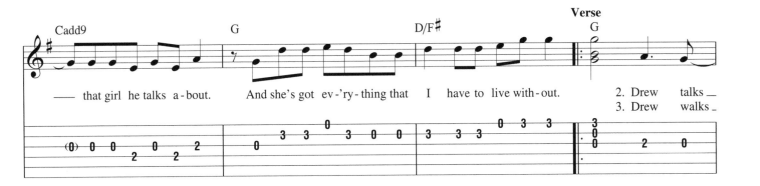

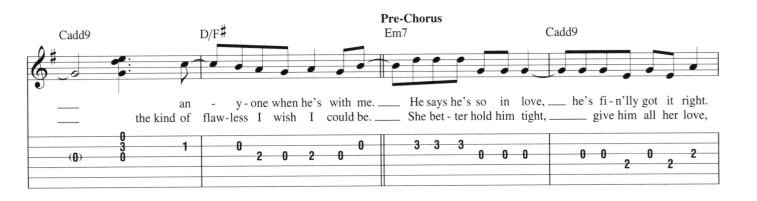

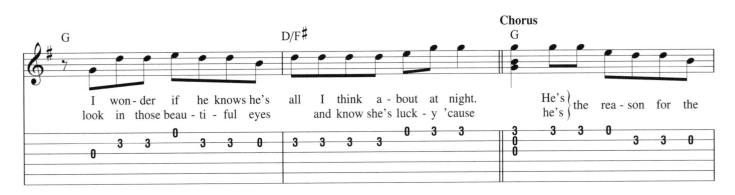

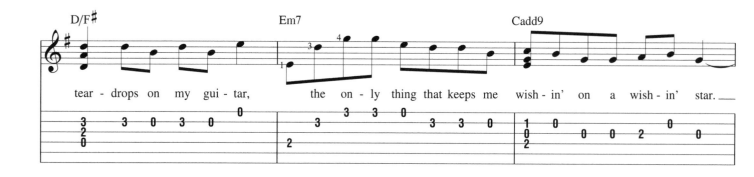

tear - drops on my gui - tar, the on - ly thing that keeps me wish - in' on a wish - in' star.

He's the song in the car I keep sing - in'. Don't know why I do.

Interlude

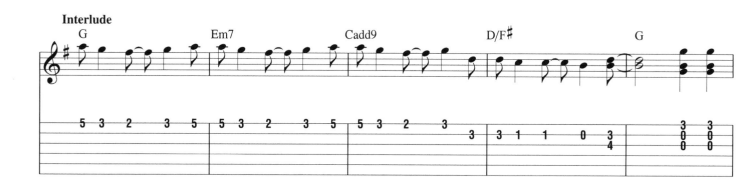

Pre-Chorus

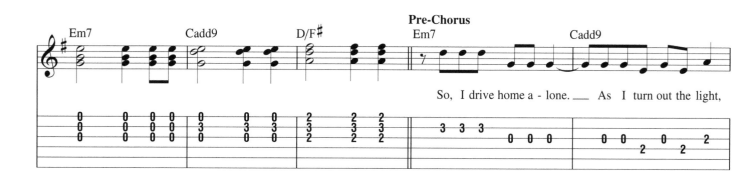

So, I drive home a - lone. As I turn out the light,

Chorus

I'll put his pic - ture down and may - be get some sleep to - night. 'Cause he's the rea - son for the

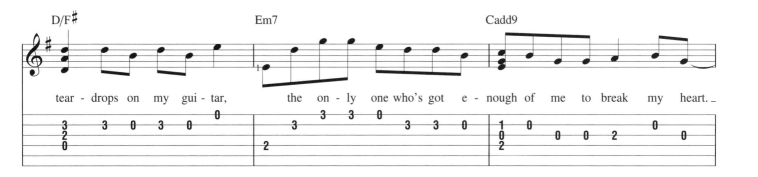

tear - drops on my gui - tar, the on - ly one who's got e - nough of me to break my heart. _

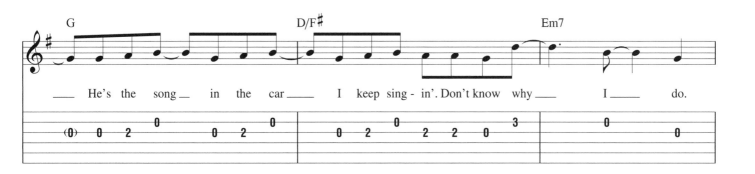

_ He's the song _ in the car _ I keep sing - in'. Don't know why _ I _ do.

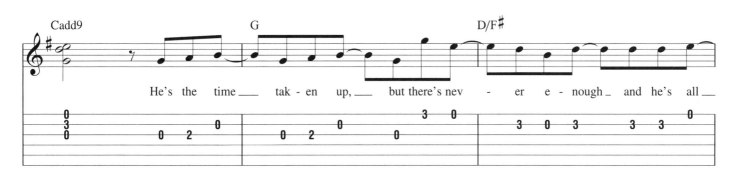

He's the time _ tak - en up, _ but there's nev - er e - nough _ and he's all _

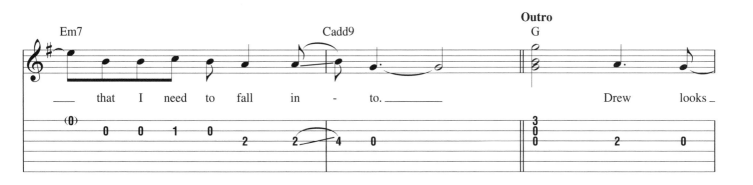

Outro

_ that I need to fall in - to. _____ Drew looks _

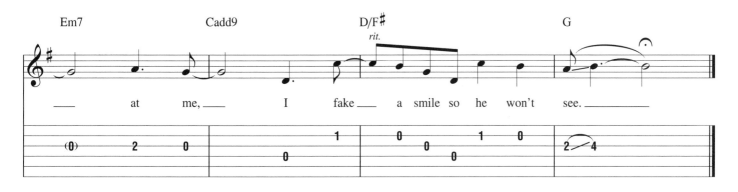

_ at me, _ I fake _ a smile so he won't see. _____

x

Thriller

Words and Music by Rod Temperton

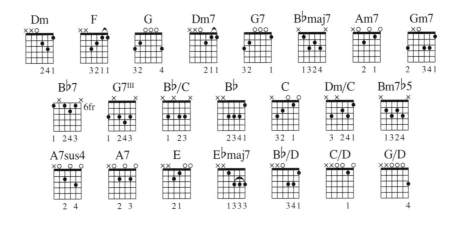

*Tune down 1/2 step:
(low to high) E♭-A♭-D♭-G♭-B♭-E♭

Strum Pattern: 3
Pick Pattern: 3

Intro

Moderate Rock

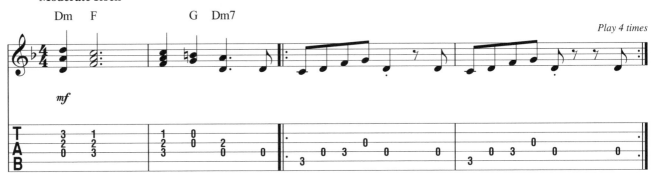

*Optional: To match recording, tune down 1/2 step.

1. It's close to mid - night, __ and some - thin' e - vil's lurk - in' in the
2. You hear the door slam __ and re - al - ize there's no - where left to
3. They're out to get you. __ There's de - mons clos - in' in on ev - 'ry

**Sung as written.

dark. _____   Un - der the moon - light _____ you
run. _____   You feel the cold hand, _____ and
side. _____   They will pos - sess you _____ un -

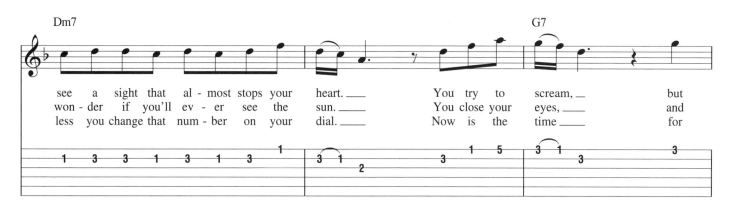

see a sight that al - most stops your heart. _____   You try to scream, _____ but
won - der if you'll ev - er see the sun. _____   You close your eyes, _____ and
less you change that num - ber on your dial. _____   Now is the time _____ for

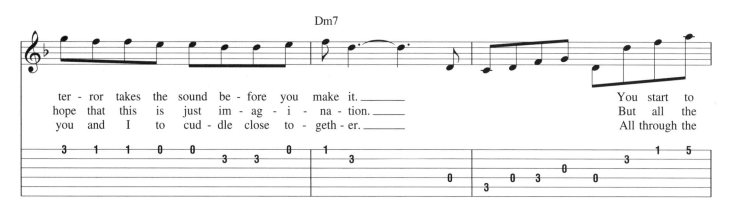

ter - ror takes the sound be - fore you make it. _____   You start to
hope that this is just im - ag - i - na - tion. _____   But all the
you and I to cud - dle close to - geth - er. _____   All through the

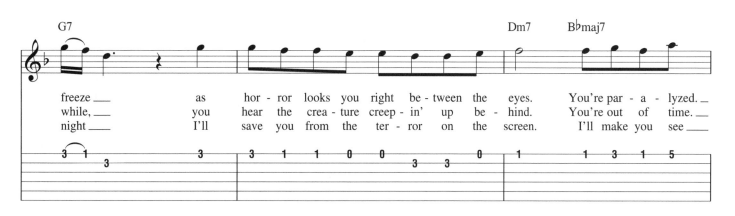

freeze _____ as hor - ror looks you right be - tween the eyes. You're par - a - lyzed. _____
while, _____ you hear the crea - ture creep - in' up be - hind. You're out of time. _____
night _____ I'll save you from the ter - ror on the screen. I'll make you see _____

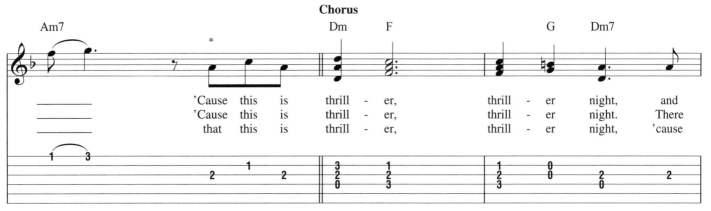

*Sung one octave higher.

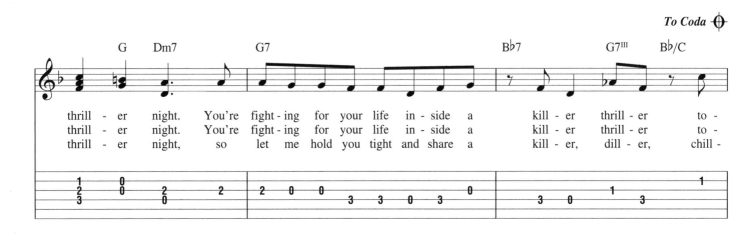

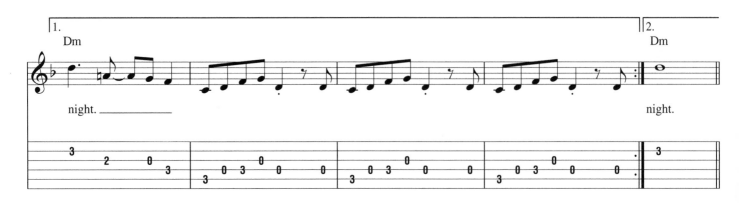

Bridge

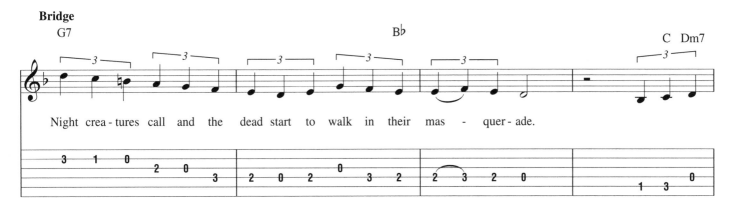

Night crea-tures call and the dead start to walk in their mas - quer-ade.

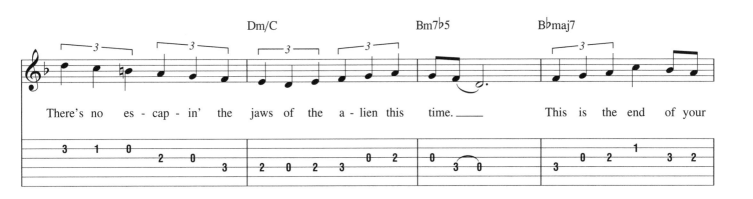

There's no es-cap - in' the jaws of the a - lien this time.____ This is the end of your

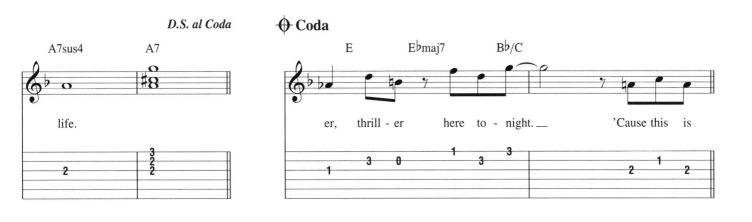

D.S. al Coda ⊕ **Coda**

life.   er, thrill - er here to - night.__ 'Cause this is

Chorus

thrill - er, thrill - er night, girl, I can thrill you more than an - y

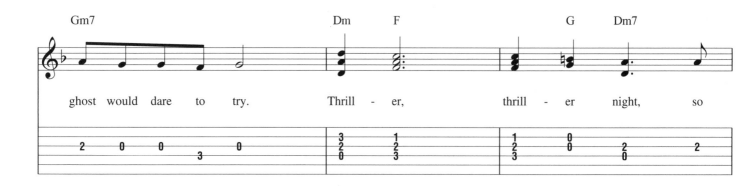

ghost would dare to try. Thrill - er, thrill - er night, so

Interlude

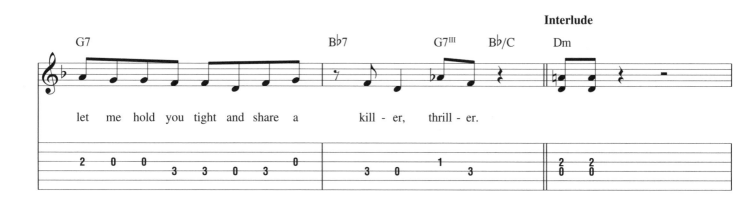

let me hold you tight and share a kill - er, thrill - er.

I'm gon - na thrill you to -

Outro

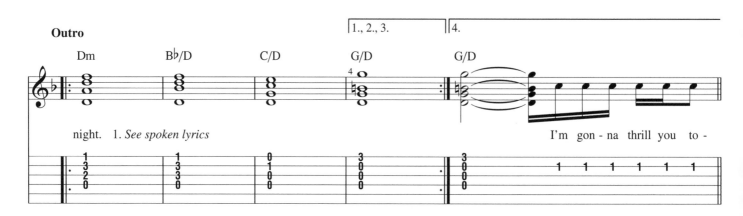

night. 1. *See spoken lyrics*

I'm gon - na thrill you to -

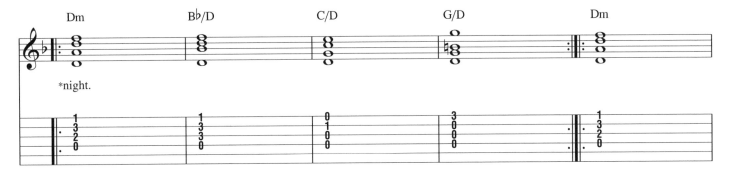

*night.

*Sung 1st time only.

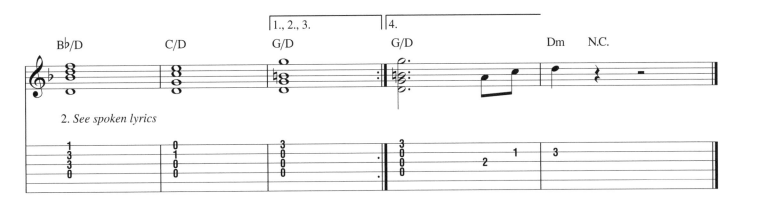

2. *See spoken lyrics*

Additional Lyrics

1. *Darkness falls across the land.*
   The midnight hour is close at hand.
   Creatures crawl in search of blood
   To terrorize y'all's neighborhood.
   And whosoever shall be found
   Without the soul for getting down
   Must stand and face the hounds of hell
   And rot inside a corpse's shell.

2. *The foulest stench is in the air,*
   The funk of forty thousand years,
   And grizzly ghouls from every tomb
   Are closing in to seal your doom.
   And though you fight to stay alive,
   Your body starts to shiver,
   For no mere mortal can resist
   The evil of the thriller.

Viva la Vida

Words and Music by Guy Berryman, Jon Buckland, Will Champion and Chris Martin

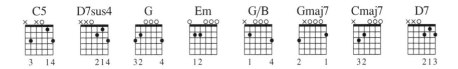

*Capo 1

Strum Pattern: 4
Pick Pattern: 5

Intro
Moderately

*Optional: To match recording, place capo at 1st fret.

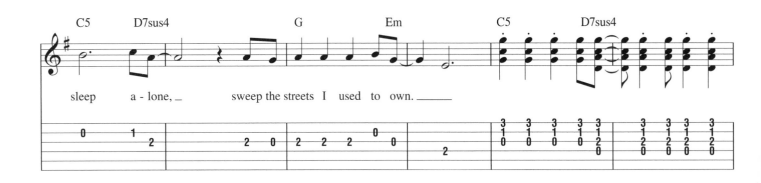

1. I used to rule the world. _ Seas would rise when I gave the word. _ Now in the morn-ing I

sleep a - lone, _ sweep the streets I used to own. _____

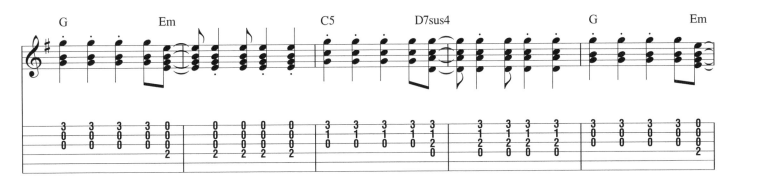

Verse

2. I used to roll the dice, _ feel the fear in the en - e-my's eyes. _____ Lis - ten as the
wild _____ wind _ blew down the doors to let me in. _ Shut-tered win-dows and the

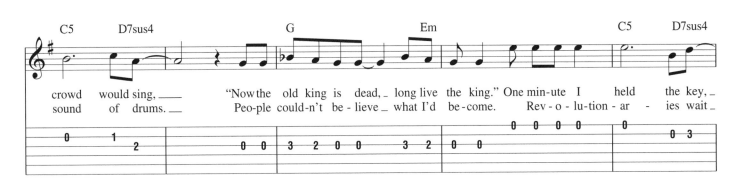

crowd would sing, _____ "Now the old king is dead, _ long live the king." One min-ute I held the key, _
sound of drums. _ Peo-ple could-n't be - lieve _ what I'd be-come. Rev - o - lu-tion - ar - ies wait _

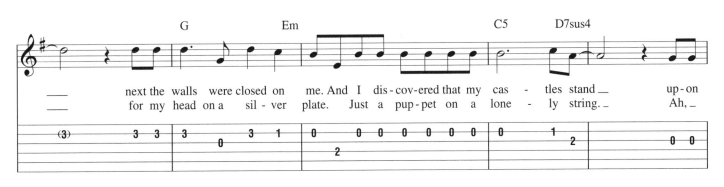

_____ next the walls were closed on me. And I dis-cov-ered that my cas - tles stand _ up-on
_____ for my head on a sil - ver plate. Just a pup-pet on a lone - ly string. _ Ah, _

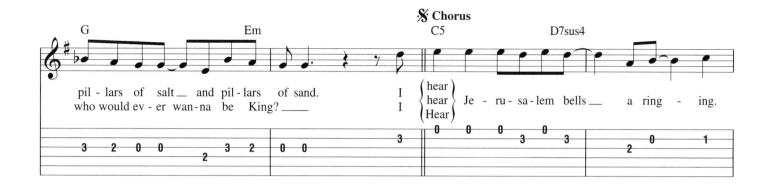

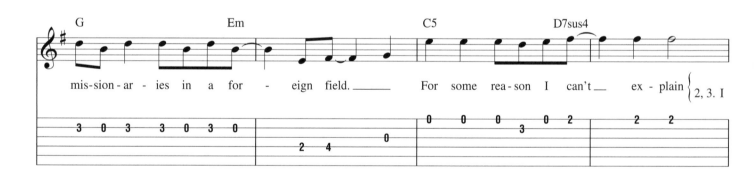

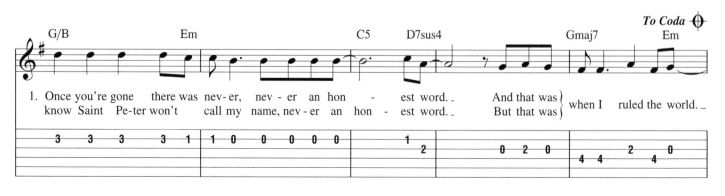

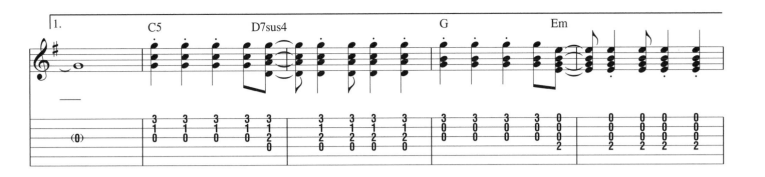

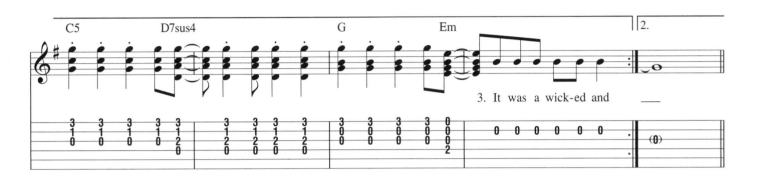

3. It was a wick-ed and

Interlude

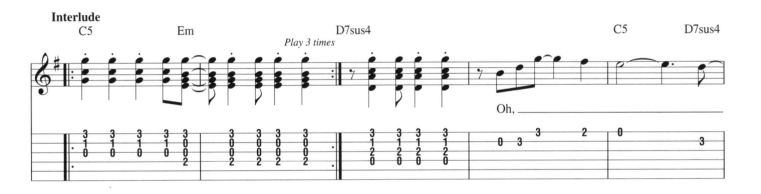

Oh,

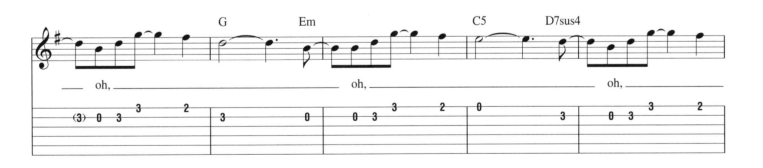

oh, oh, oh,

D.S. al Coda

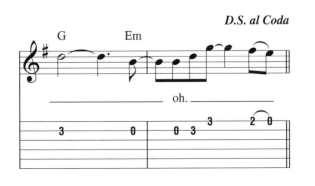

oh.

Coda

Repeat and fade

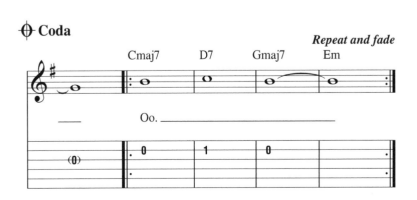

Oo.

We're Not Gonna Take It

Words and Music by Daniel Dee Snider

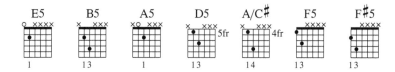

Strum Pattern: 1, 2

Intro

Moderate Rock

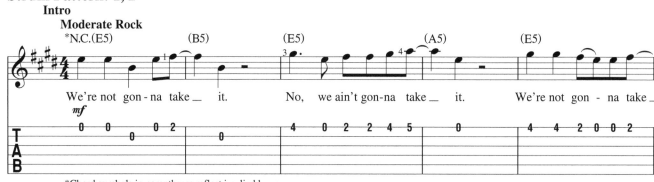

*Chord symbols in parentheses reflect implied harmony.

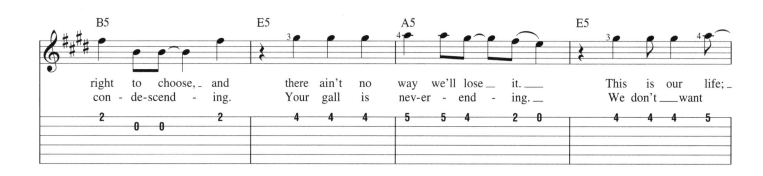

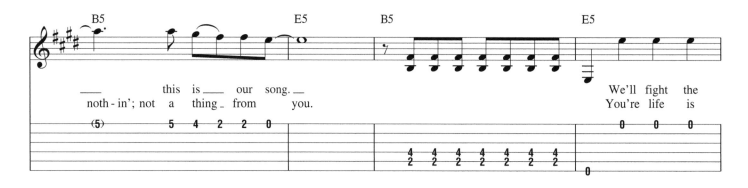

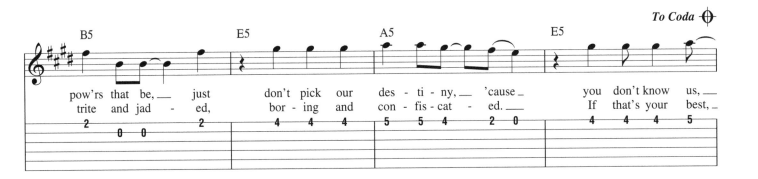

pow'rs that be, ___ just   don't pick our   des - ti - ny, ___ 'cause ___   you don't know us, ___
trite and jad - ed,   bor - ing and   con - fis - cat - ed. ___   If   that's your best, _

Chorus

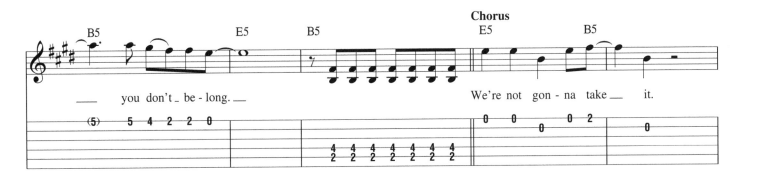

___ you don't _ be - long. ___   We're not gon - na take ___ it.

D.S. al Coda

No, we ain't gon-na take ___ it.   We're not gon - na take ___ it   an - y - more. ___

⊕ **Coda**

Bridge

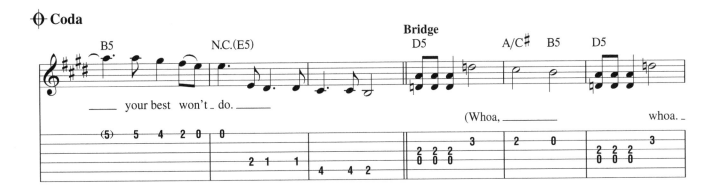

___ your best won't _ do. ___   (Whoa, ___   whoa. _

We're right,   we're free,   we'll fight.   You'll see. ___   Whoa!
Yeah! _   Yeah! _   Yeah! _   Yeah!) ___

Chorus

We're not gon-na take ___ it. No, we ain't gon-na take ___ it. We're not gon-na take ___

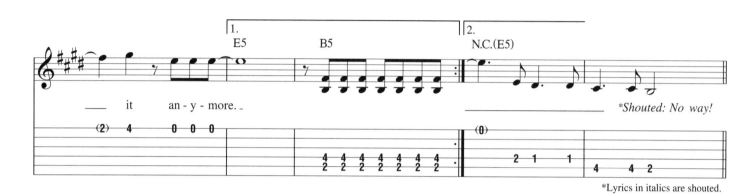

___ it an-y-more. ___

Shouted: No way!

*Lyrics in italics are shouted.

Guitar Solo

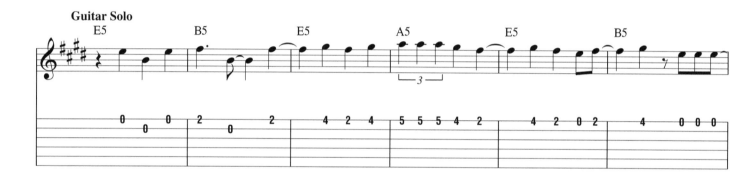

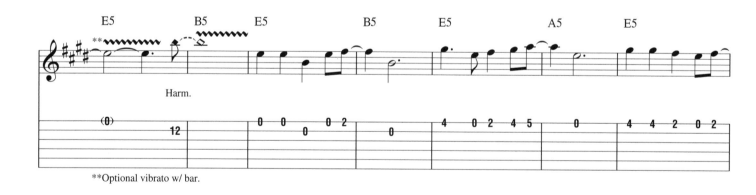

Harm.

**Optional vibrato w/ bar.

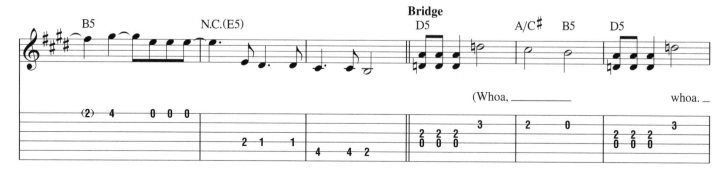

Bridge

(Whoa, ___ whoa. ___

We're right, we're free, we'll fight. You'll see. _____
Yeah! _ Yeah! _ Yeah! _

Breakdown-Chorus

We're not gon - na take __ it. No, we ain't gon-na take __ it. We're not gon - na take _

Outro-Chorus

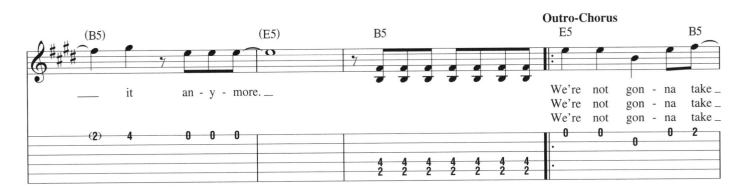

__ it an - y - more. _

We're not gon - na take _
We're not gon - na take _
We're not gon - na take _

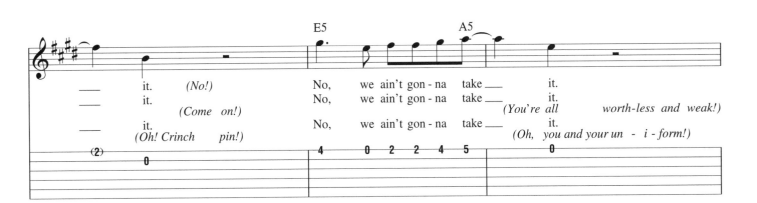

__ it. *(No!)* No, we ain't gon - na take __ it.
(Come on!) No, we ain't gon - na take __ it. *(You're all worth-less and weak!)*
__ it. *(Oh! Crinch pin!)* No, we ain't gon - na take __ it. *(Oh, you and your un - i - form!)*

Repeat and fade

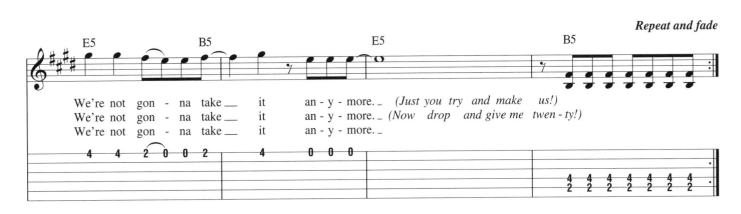

We're not gon - na take __ it an - y - more. _ *(Just you try and make us!)*
We're not gon - na take __ it an - y - more. _ *(Now drop and give me twen - ty!)*
We're not gon - na take __ it an - y - more. _

When You Were Young

Words and Music by Brandon Flowers, Dave Keuning, Mark Stoermer and Ronnie Vannucci

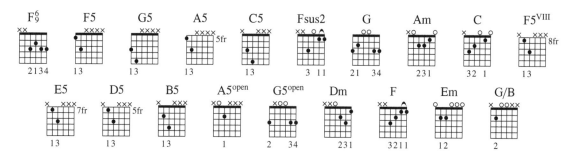

*Tune down 1/2 step:
(low to high) E♭-A♭-D♭-G♭-B♭-E♭

Strum Pattern: 1
Pick Pattern: 5

Intro
Moderate Rock

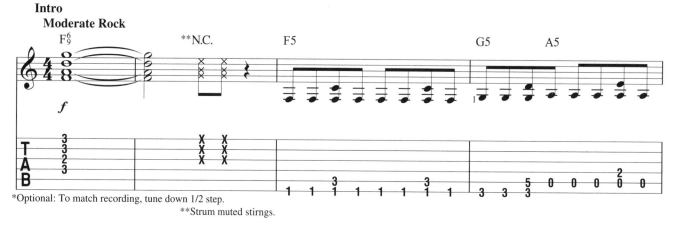

*Optional: To match recording, tune down 1/2 step.
**Strum muted stirngs.

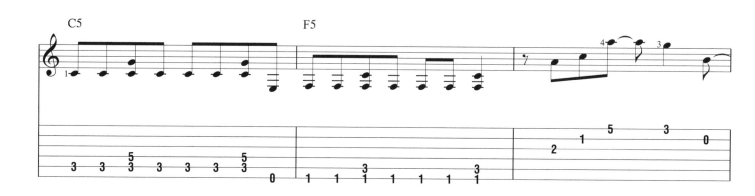

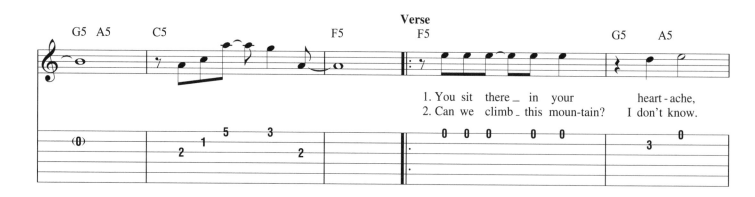

1. You sit there _ in your   heart - ache,
2. Can we climb _ this moun-tain?   I don't know.

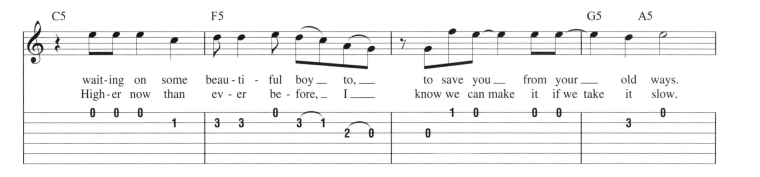

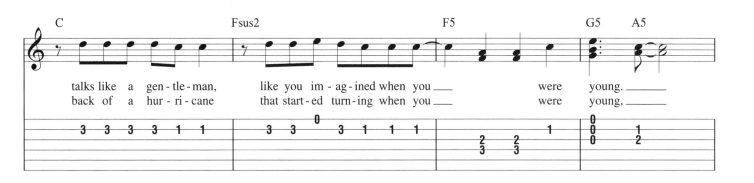

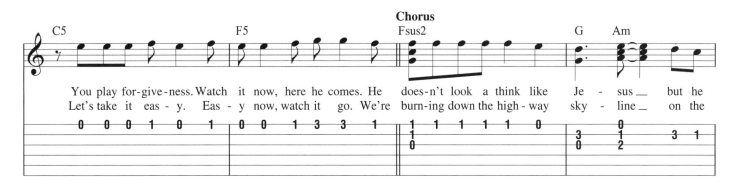

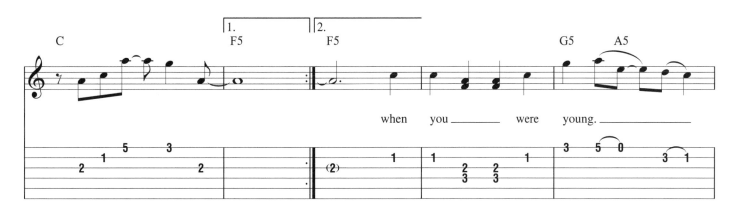

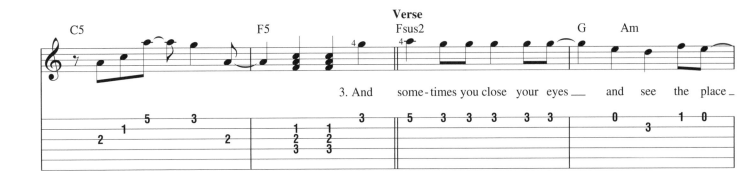

Verse

3. And some-times you close your eyes ___ and see the place ___

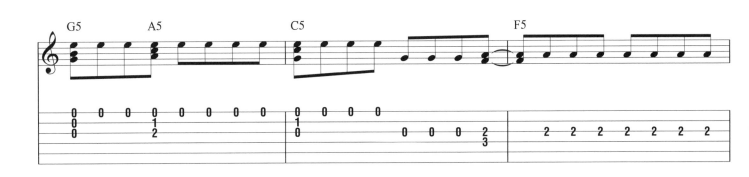

___ where you used to live ___ when you ___ were young.

Interlude

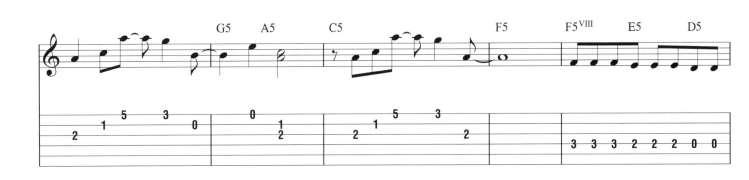

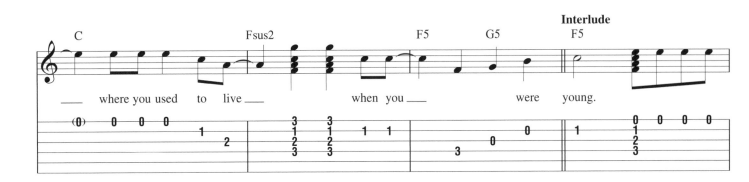

Bridge

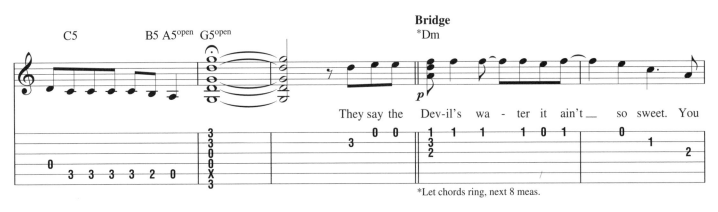

They say the Dev-il's wa - ter it ain't ___ so sweet. You

*Let chords ring, next 8 meas.

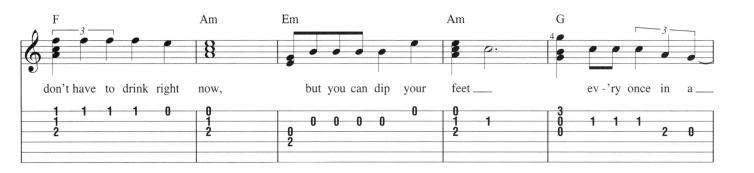

don't have to drink right now, but you can dip your feet_____ ev-'ry once in a_____

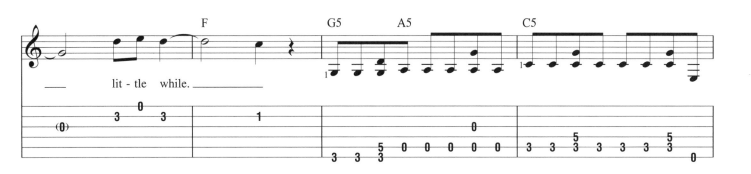

_____ lit - tle while. _____

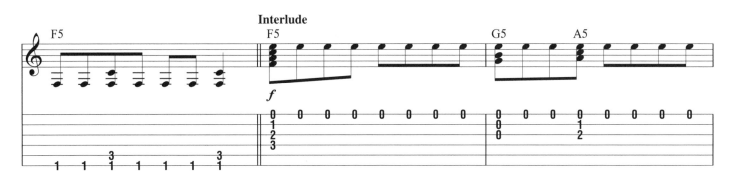

Interlude

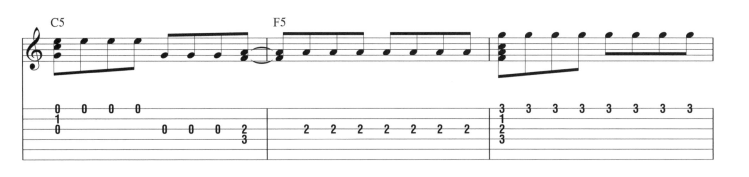

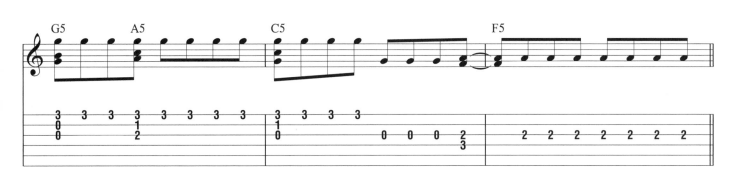

Verse

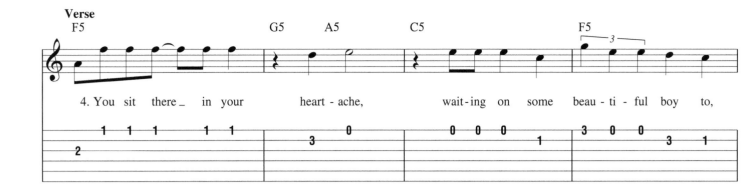

4. You sit there _ in your heart - ache, wait-ing on some beau - ti - ful boy to,

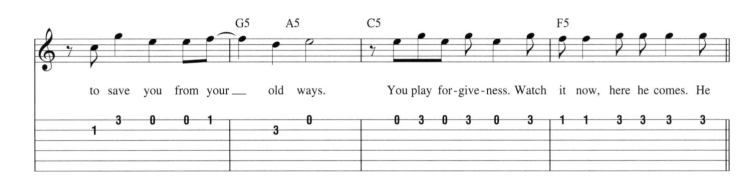

to save you from your _ old ways. You play for-give-ness. Watch it now, here he comes. He

Outro-Chorus

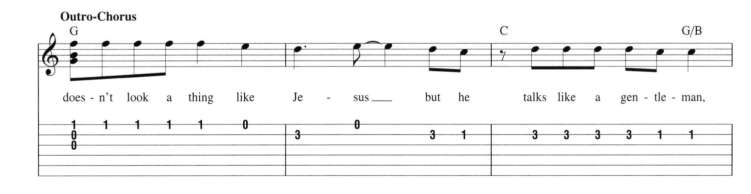

does - n't look a thing like Je - sus _ but he talks like a gen - tle - man,

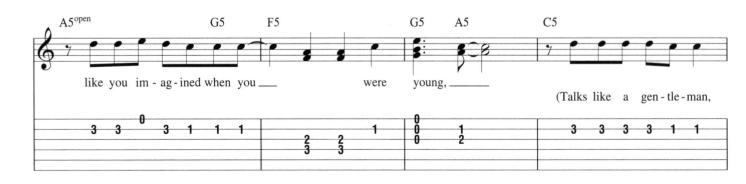

like you im - ag - ined when you _ were young, _

(Talks like a gen - tle - man,

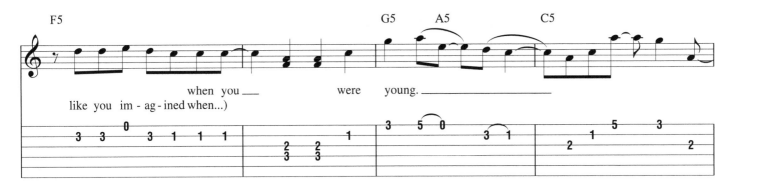

when you ___ were young. _____
(like you im - ag - ined when...)

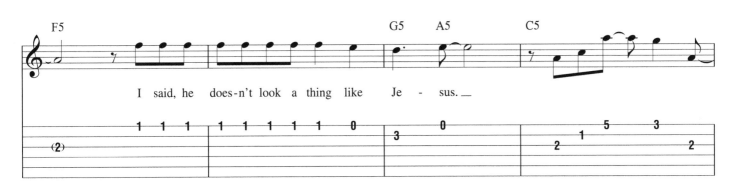

I said, he does-n't look a thing like Je - sus. __

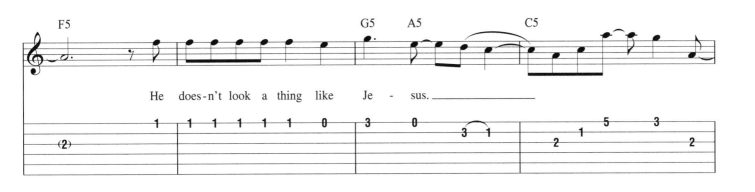

He does-n't look a thing like Je - sus. _____

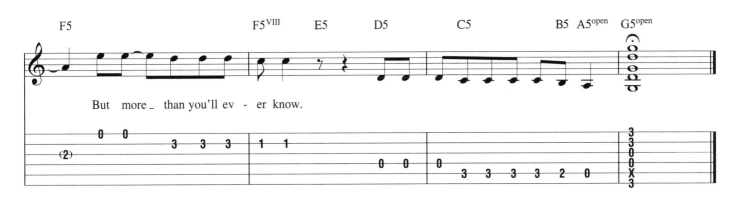

But more _ than you'll ev - er know.

White Wedding

Words and Music by Billy Idol

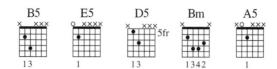

Strum Pattern: 1

Intro
Moderately fast Rock

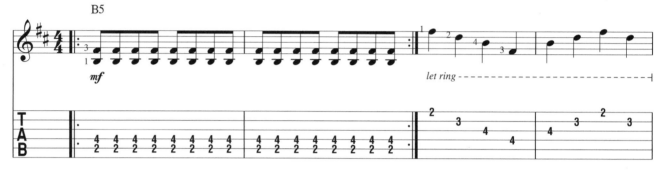

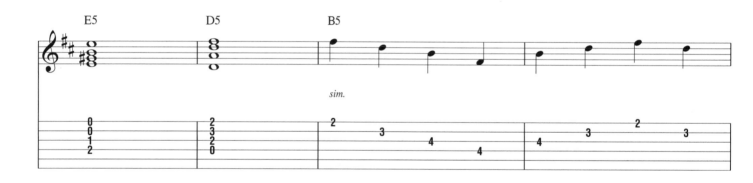

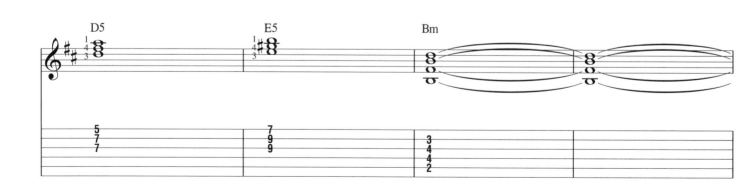

Verse

1. Hey, lit-tle sis-ter, what have you done? _
2., 3. *See additional lyrics*

Hey, lit-tle sis-ter, who's _ the on - ly one? _

Hey, lit-tle sis-ter, who's _ your su - per - man?

Hey, lit-tle sis-ter, who's _ the one _ you want? Hey, lit-tle sis-ter, shot - gun! It's a

Chorus

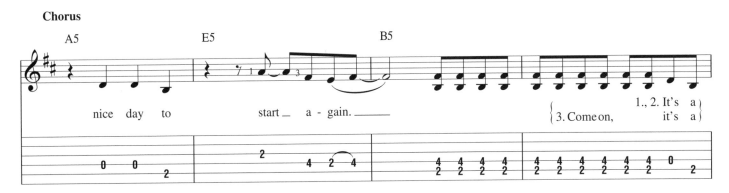

nice day to start _ a - gain. _

1., 2. It's a
3. Come on, it's a

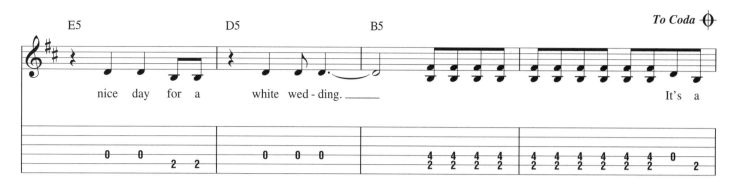

nice day for a white wed-ding. _____ It's a

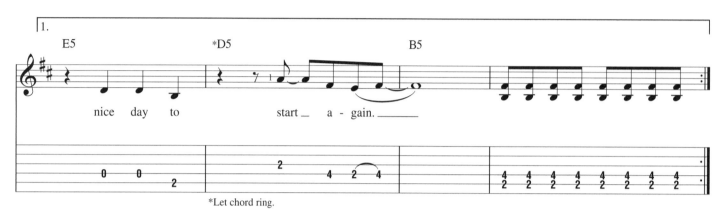

1.

nice day to start _ a-gain. _____

*Let chord ring.

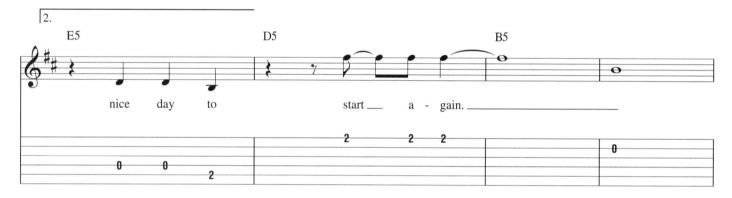

2.

nice day to start _ a-gain. _____

Interlude

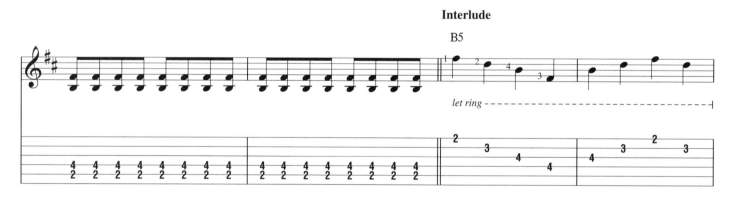

let ring -

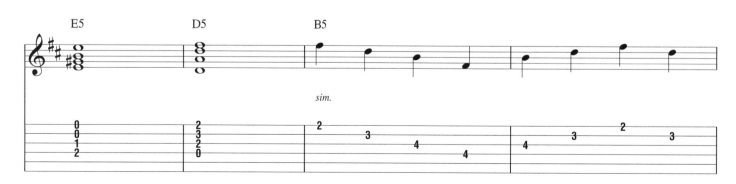

sim.

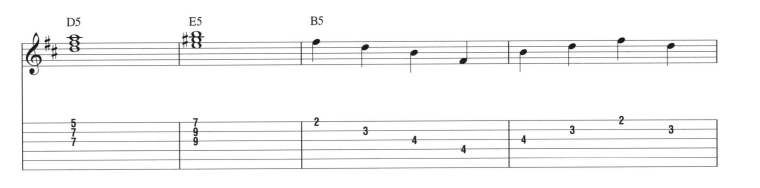

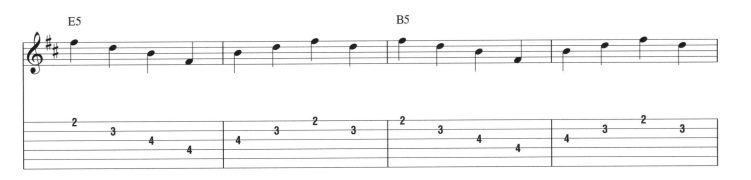

Spoken: Pick it up.

D.S. al Coda

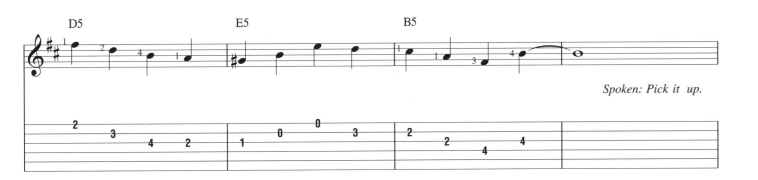

Take ___ me back home, yeah.

⊕ Coda

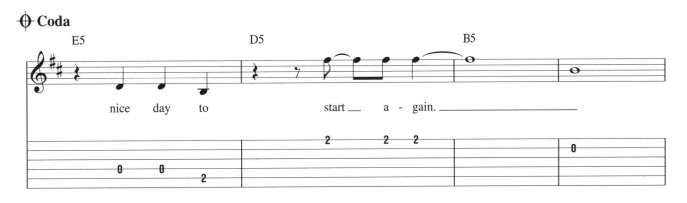

nice day to   start ___ a - gain. _____

Bridge

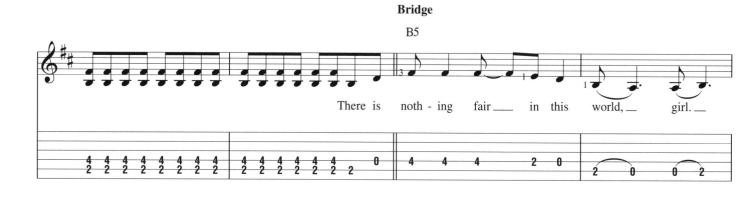

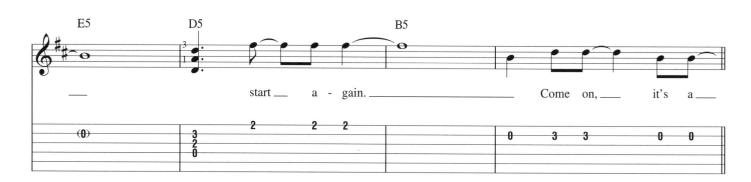

Outro-Chorus

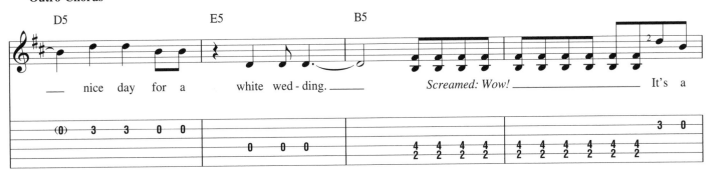

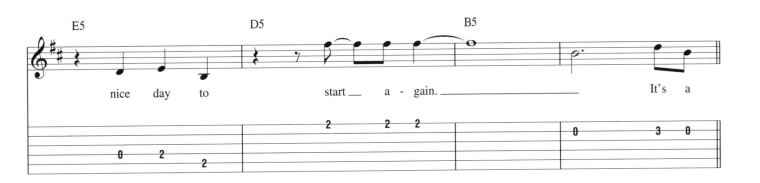

Additional Lyrics

2. Hey little sister, who is it you're with?
   Hey little sister, what's your fascination?
   Hey little sister, shotgun, oh, yeah.
   Hey little sister, who's your superman?
   Hey little sister, shotgun!

3. Hey little sister, what have you done?
   Hey little sister, who's the only one?
   I've been away for so long.
   I've been away for so long.
   I let you go for so long.

All Day and All of the Night

Words and Music by Ray Davies

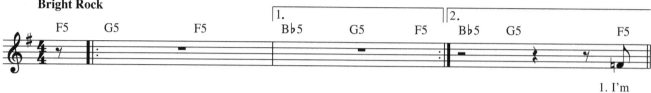

Strum Pattern: 2
Pick Pattern: 6

Intro
Bright Rock

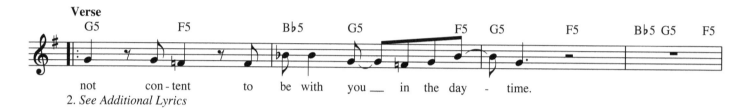

1. I'm

Verse

not con-tent to be with you ___ in the day - time.
2. See Additional Lyrics

Girl, I want to be with you ___ all of the time. The

Pre-Chorus **Chorus**

on - ly time I feel all right ___ is by your ___ side. _____ Girl, I want to

be with you ___ all of the ___ time, all day and all of the night. ___ All day and

all of the night. ___ All day and all of the night. ___

Additional Lyrics

2. I believe that you and me last forever.
   Oh yeah, all day and night time, yours; leave me never.

Angel of the Morning

Words and Music by Chip Taylor

Bridge

me, through the tears of ___ the day, ___ of ___ the years,

Chorus

ba - by. Just call me an-gel of the morn - ing, an - gel, just touch my cheek be-fore you

leave me, { ba - by. / dar - ling. } leave me, dar - ling. _____

Repeat and fade

Outro

Additional Lyrics

2. Maybe the sun's light will be dim,
And it won't matter anyhow;
If morning's echo says we've sinned,
Well, it was what I wanted now.
And if we're victims of the night,
I won't be blinded by the light.

Bang a Gong (Get It On)

Words and Music by Marc Bolan

Strum Pattern: 3
Pick Pattern: 3

𝄋 Verse
Moderate Rock

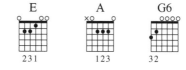

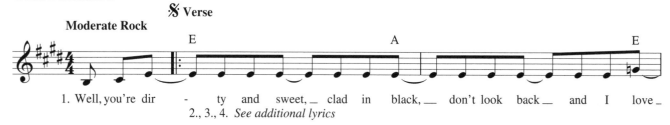

1. Well, you're dir - ty and sweet, ___ clad in black, ___ don't look back ___ and I love ___
2., 3., 4. *See additional lyrics*

___ you. You're dir - ty and sweet, ___ oh yeah. ___ Well, you're slim ___

___ and you're weak, ___ you've got the teeth of a hy - dra up - on ___ you. You're

dir - ty, sweet and you're my girl. ___   Get it on, _____ bang a gong. ___

To Coda ⊕

___ Get it on. ___   Get it on, _____ bang a gong. ___ Get it on. ___

1., 2.   *3.*

___   2. Well, you're built ___

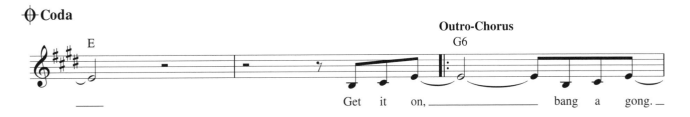

D.S. al Coda

4. Well, you're dir -

⊕ **Coda**

Outro-Chorus

___   Get it on, _____ bang a gong. ___

Repeat and fade

___ Get it on. _____   Get it on, ___

Additional Lyrics

2. Well, you're built like a car;
   You've got a hub cap diamond star halo.
   You're built like a car, oh yeah.
   Well, you're an untamed youth,
   That's the truth, with your cloak full of eagles.
   You're dirty, sweet and you're my girl.

3. Well, you're windy and wild.
   You've got the blues in your shoes and your stockings.
   You're windy and wild, oh yeah.
   Well, you're built like a car;
   You've got a hub cap diamond star halo.
   You're dirty, sweet and you're my girl.

4. Well, you're dirty and sweet.
   Clad in black, don't look back and I love you.
   You're dirty and sweet, oh yeah.
   Well, you dance when you walk.
   So let's dance, take a chance, understand me.
   You're dirty, sweet and you're my girl.

Born Under a Bad Sign

Words and Music by Booker T. Jones and William Bell

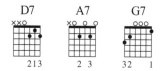

Strum Pattern: 1
Pick Pattern: 2

Chorus
Moderately

Born un-der a bad sign.   Been down _ since I be-gan to crawl. _

If it was-n't for bad luck,   you know I would-n't have no luck at all.

Verse

1. Hard luck and trou-ble   been my on-ly friend.   I been on my own
2., 3. *See additional lyrics*

1., 2.   **3.**

D.C. al Coda   **Coda**

ev-er since I ___ was ten.   to my grave. _

Additional Lyrics

2. I can't read, I didn't learn how to write.
   My whole life has been one big fight.

3. You know wine and women is all I crave.
   A big leg woman gonna carry me to my grave.

Breathe

Words and Music by Holly Lamar and Stephanie Bentley

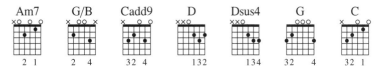

Strum Pattern: 6
Pick Pattern: 4

Intro
Moderately slow, in 2

let ring throughout

1. I can feel the mag-

-ic float - ing in _____ the air. _____ Be - ing _____ with

you gets me that _____ way. I watch the sun-

-light dance a - cross _____ your face, _____ and I _____

nev - er been this swept a - way.

Verse

2. All my thoughts just seem to set - tle on ____ the breeze ____
3. *See additional lyrics*

when I'm ly - in' wrapped ___ up in your arms.

The whole world just fades a - way, ___ the on - ly thing ___

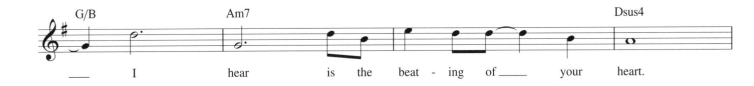

___ I hear is the beat - ing of ___ your heart.

Chorus

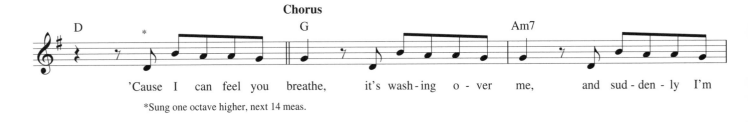

'Cause I can feel you breathe, it's wash-ing o - ver me, and sud - den - ly I'm

*Sung one octave higher, next 14 meas.

melt - ing in - to you. There's noth - ing left to prove, ba - by, all we

need is just ___ to be ___ caught ___ up in the

Additional Lyrics

3. In a way I know my heart is waking up
   As all the walls come tumbling down.
   Closer than I've ever felt before,
   And I know and you know
   There's no need for words right now.

Centerfold

Written by Seth Justman

Strum Pattern: 4
Pick Pattern: 6

Intro
Moderate Funk

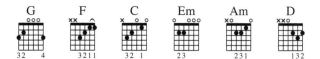

play 4 times

G ... F ... C

Na, na, na, na, na, na, na, na, na, na, na, na, na, na, na, na.

Verse

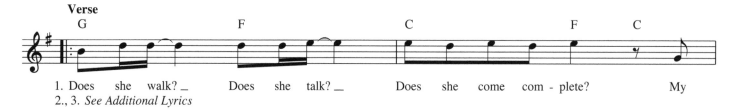

G ... F ... C ... F ... C

1. Does she walk? _ Does she talk? _ Does she come com-plete? My
2., 3. *See Additional Lyrics*

G ... F ... C ... F ... C

home-room, home-room an-gel al-ways pulled me from my seat.

G ... F ... C ... F ... C

She was pure like snow-flakes no one could ev-er stain; ___ the

G ... F ... C

mem-o-ry of my an-gel could nev-er cause ___ me pain. The

Em ... Am ... C ... D

years go by; I'm look-in' through _ a gir-ly mag-a-zine; and

To Coda ⊕

Em ... Am ... C ... D

there's my home-room an-gel on the pag-es in be-tween. My

Chorus

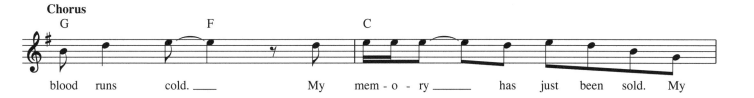

blood runs cold. _____ My mem - o - ry _____ has just been sold. My

an - gel is the cen - ter-fold, an - gel is the cen - ter-fold. My blood runs cold. _ My

2nd time, D.C. al Coda
(take repeat)

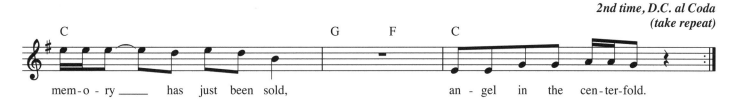

mem-o - ry _____ has just been sold, an - gel in the cen-ter-fold.

✛ *Coda*

Na, na, na, na, na, na, na, na, na, na, na, na, na, na, na, na. _____ My

Outro-Chorus

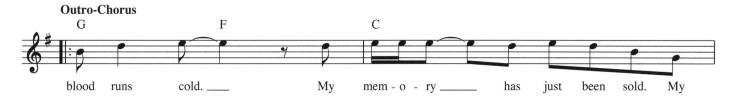

blood runs cold. _____ My mem - o - ry _____ has just been sold. My

Repeat and Fade

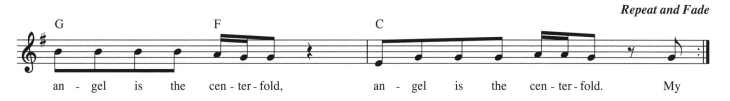

an - gel is the cen - ter-fold, an - gel is the cen - ter-fold. My

Additional Lyrics

2. Slipped me notes under the desk
   While I was thinkin' about her dress.
   I was shy, I turned away before she caught my eye.
   I was shakin' in my shoes
   Whenever she flashed those baby blues.
   Something had a hold on me when angel passed close by.
   Those soft, fuzzy sweaters, too magical to touch;
   To see her in that negligee is really just too much.

3. It's okay, I understand this ain't no never-never land.
   I hope that when this issue's gone,
   I'll see you when your clothes are on.
   Take your car, yes, we will. We'll take your car and drive it.
   Take it to a motel room and take 'em off in private.
   A part of me has just been ripped.
   The pages from my mind are stripped.
   Ah, no! I can't deny it. Oh yeah! I guess I gotta buy it.

Crying

Words and Music by Roy Orbison and Joe Melson

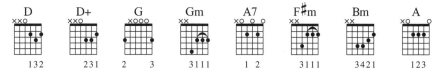

Strum Pattern: 2
Pick Pattern: 4

Intro   Verse

Moderately

1. I was all right   for a - while;   I could

smile   for a - while, _____   but I saw you last night;_ you held my

hand so tight, _   as you stopped   to say, _ "Hel - lo."   Oh, you

wished   me   well; _   you _____ could - n't tell _   that I'd been

Chorus

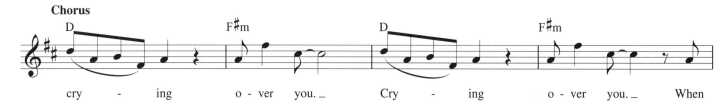

cry - ing   o - ver you. _   Cry - ing   o - ver you. _   When

you   said, "So long;"   left me stand - ing _____ all a - lone, _   a - lone and

cry - ing, _____   cry - ing, _____   cry - ing, _____   cry - ing. It's hard to

Every Breath You Take

Music and Lyrics by Sting

Additional Lyrics

2. Ev'ry single day, ev'ry word you say,
   Ev'ry game you play, ev'ry night you stay,
   I'll be watching you.

Good Morning Little Schoolgirl

Words and Music by Willie Williamson

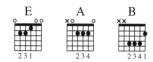

Strum Pattern: 1, 6
Pick Pattern: 1, 3
Intro
Bright Rock

Oh, oh, oh, oh, oh.

Oh, oh, oh, oh, oh.   Oh, oh, oh, oh, oh.

Oh, oh, oh, oh, oh.   Oh, oh, oh.   Oh, oh, oh, oh, oh.

%. **Verse**

1., 3. Good morn - in' lit - tle school - girl. _   Good morn - in' lit - tle school - girl. _
2., 4. *See Additional Lyrics*

Can I _____ go _ home with, _   a-won't you let me go _ home with you, _ so I can

To Coda ⊕

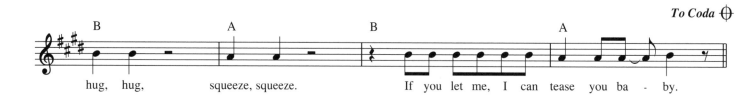

hug, hug,   squeeze, squeeze.   If you let me, I can tease you ba - by.

Chorus

Hey,   hey, ___   hey, hey,   hey, ___   hey,   h - hey,   hey. ___

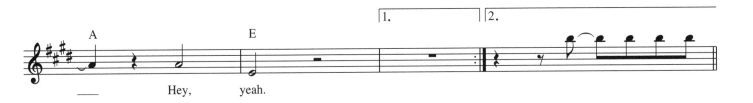

___   Hey,   yeah.

Guitar Solo

D.S. al Coda
(take repeat)

$\oplus$ *Coda*
Outro

Repeat and Fade

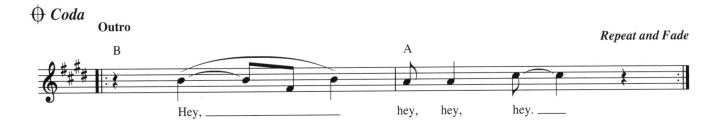

Hey, ___   hey,   hey,   hey. ___

Additional Lyrics

Let's dance, little schoolgirl.
Let's dance, little schoolgirl.
Won't you let me take you to the hop, hop;
Have a party at the soda shop,
So we can do the twist, do the stroll,
To the music of the rock and roll, oh.

Good mornin' little schoolgirl.
Good mornin' little schoolgirl.
Can I go home with,
A-won't you let me go home with you?
Tell your mama and your papa that I love you.
Tell your sisters and your brother that I love you.

I Am a Man of Constant Sorrow

featured in O BROTHER, WHERE ART THOU?

Words and Music by Carter Stanley

Strum Pattern: 3, 5
Pick Pattern: 1, 4

Intro
Moderately, in 2

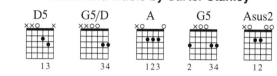

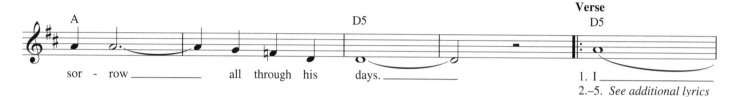

In con - stant

sor - row _____ all through his days. _____

Verse
1. I _____
2.–5. *See additional lyrics*

_____ am a man _____ of con - stant sor - row. _____ I've seen trou-

- ble all my days. I _____ bid fare - well _____

_____ to old _ Ken - tuck-y, _____ the place _ where I _____ was born and

1.–4.

raised. The place where he _____ was born and raised. _____

5.

shore.

Additional Lyrics

2. For six long years I've been in trouble,
   No pleasure here on earth I've found.
   For in this world I'm bound to ramble;
   I have no friends to help me now.
   He has no friends to help him now.

3. It's fare thee well, my own true lover,
   I never expect to see you again,
   For I'm bound to ride that Northern railroad;
   Perhaps I'll die upon this train.
   Perhaps he'll die upon this train.

4. You can bury me in some deep valley,
   For many years where I may lay,
   And you may learn to love another
   While I am sleeping in my grave.
   While he is sleeping in his grave.

5. Maybe your friends think I'm just a stranger;
   My face, you never will see no more.
   But there is one promise that is given:
   I'll meet you on God's golden shore.
   He'll meet you on God's golden shore.

One Bourbon, One Scotch, One Beer

Words and Music by John Lee Hooker

Strum Pattern: 3, 4
Pick Pattern: 1, 3

Chorus
Moderate Blues Shuffle

One bour-bon, one scotch and one beer. One

bour-bon, one scotch and one beer.

Verse

1. Hey, mis-ter bar-ten-der come in here! I want an-oth-er drink and I
3. *See Additional Lyrics*

want it now. My ba-by she's gone, she's been gone to-night; I

ain't seen ma ba-by since night be-fore last. Ah, one bour-bon, one scotch and one

Verse

beer.

2. *Spoken: And then I sat there,*
4. *See Additional Lyrics*

get-tin' high,

mel-low,   knocked out,   feel-in' good.   And by that time,

I   looked on the wall   at the old   clock on the wall.   By that time, __

__   it was   ten-thir-ty then.   I looked down at the bar

at the bar - ten-der.   Said...   He said, "What do ya want _ John-ny?"   One

Chorus

G7

1.   2.

D.C. and Fade

bour-bon,   one   scotch   and one   beer.

Additional Lyrics

3. Well my baby's been gone, she's been gone tonight
   I ain't seen my baby since night before last.
   I wanna get drunk, get her off a' my mind.

4. *Spoken: And I sat there, gettin' high, stoned, knocked out,*
   And by that time, I looked on the wall,
   At the old clock again, and by that time,
   It was quarter to two:
   Last call for alcohol.
   I said, "Hey Mr. Bartender!"
   "What do ya want?"

I Saw the Light

Words and Music by Hank Williams

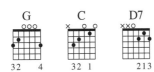

Strum Pattern: 1, 3
Pick Pattern: 2, 4

1. I wan-dered so aim-less, life filled with sin.
2., 3. *See additional lyrics*

I would-n't let my dear Sav-ior in. Then Je - sus

came like a strang-er in the night. Praise the Lord, _____

Chorus
I saw the light. I saw the light, _____

I saw the light, _____ no more in dark - ness, no more in

night. _____ Now I'm so hap - py, no sor - row in sight. _____

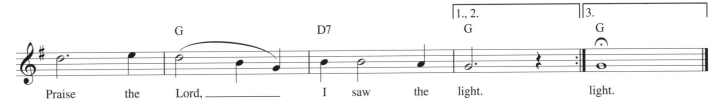

Praise the Lord, _____ I saw the light. light.

Additional Lyrics

2. Just like a blind man I wandered along,
   Worries and fears I claimed for my own.
   Then like the blind man
   That God gave back his sight.

3. I was a fool to wander and stray,
   Straight is the gate and narrow is the way.
   Now I have traded the wrong for the right.
   Praise the Lord, I saw the light.

I Want You to Want Me

Words and Music by Rick Nielsen

Additional Lyrics

Chorus 2. I want you to want me.
　　　　 I need you to need me.
　　　　 I'd love you to love me.

I'm Your Hoochie Coochie Man

Written by Willie Dixon

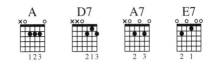

Strum Pattern: 9
Pick Pattern: 9

Verse
Moderately

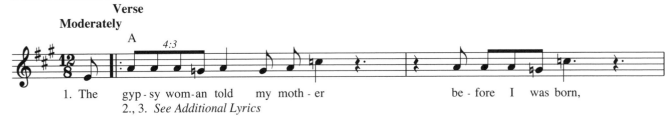

1. The gyp-sy wom-an told my moth-er be-fore I was born,
2., 3. *See Additional Lyrics*

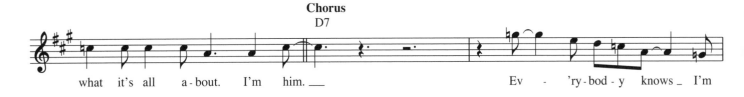

"You got a boy child com-in', goin' be a son of a gun." _

Gon-na make pret-ty wom-en ___ jump and shout, _ then the world gon-na know

Chorus

what it's all a-bout. I'm him. ___ Ev - 'ry-bod-y knows _ I'm

him. I'm the Hooch - ie Cooch-ie Man, _

ev-'ry-bod-y knows _ I'm him. | **1., 2.** | **3.** 2. I him.

Additional Lyrics

2. I got a black cat bone,
   I got a mojo too,
   I got the Johnny conkeroo,
   I'm gonna mess with you.
   I'm gonna make you girls
   Lead me by the hand,
   Then the world's gonna know,
   I'm that Hoochie Coochie Man.

3. On the seventh hour,
   On the seventh day,
   On the seventh month,
   The seventh doctor said:
   "He was born for good luck,"
   And that, you'll see,
   I got seven hundred dollars,
   Don't you mess with me.

Piece of My Heart

Words and Music by Bert Berns and Jerry Ragovoy

Strum Pattern: 4, 5
Pick Pattern: 4, 5

Verse
Slowly

1.Did-n't I make you feel like you ___ were the on - ly man?_

Did - n't I give you ev - 'ry-thing that a wom - an pos - si - bly can? _____

But with all the love I give you, it's nev - er e - nough. _ But

I'm gon - na show you, ba - by, _____ that a wom - an can be tough. _ So

Chorus

go on, go on, go on, go on, take it! Take an-oth-er lit-tle piece of my

heart now ba - by. _____ Break it! Break an - oth - er lit - tle piece of my

heart now hon - ey. _____ Have a, have an - oth - er lit - tle piece of my

To Coda

heart now, ba - by. _____ You know you got it if it makes you feel good. _ 2. You're

Spinning Wheel

Words and Music by David Clayton Thomas

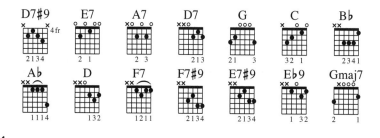

Strum Pattern: 4
Pick Pattern: 1

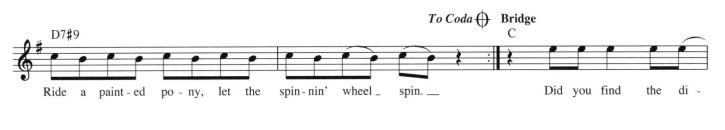

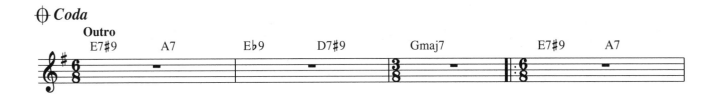

Additional Lyrics

2. Ya' got no money and ya', ya' got no home.
Spinnin' wheel, all alone.
Talkin' 'bout your troubles and ya', ya' never learn.
Ride a painted pony, let the spinnin' wheel turn.

3. Someone is waitin' just for you.
Spinnin' wheel, spinnin' true.
Drop all your troubles by the riverside.
Catch a painted pony on the spinnin' wheel ride.

The Keeper of the Stars

Words and Music by Karen Staley, Danny Mayo and Dickey Lee

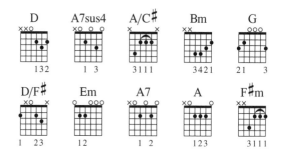

Strum Pattern: 6
Pick Pattern: 4

Intro
Moderately slow

Verse

1. It was _ no ac - ci - dent, _   me find - ing you.
2. *See additional lyrics*

Some - one _ had a hand in it _   long be - fore _ we ev - er knew.

Now I _ just can't _ be - lieve _   you're in _ my life.

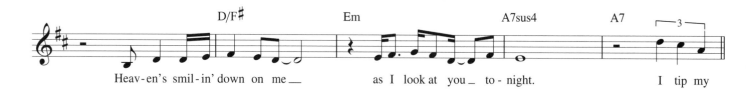

Heav - en's smil - in' down on me _ as I look at you _ to - night.   I tip my

Chorus

hat to the Keep - er of ___ the Stars. He sure knew what he ___ was

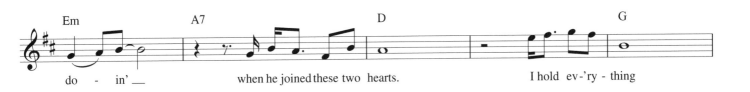

do - in' ___ when he joined these two hearts. I hold ev-'ry - thing

when I hold ___ you in my arms. I've got all ___ I'll ev - er need,

thanks to the Keep - er of ___ the Stars. _____ Stars. _____

Outro

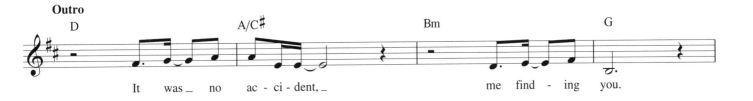

It was ___ no ac - ci - dent, ___ me find - ing you.

Some-one had a hand in it ___ long be-fore ___ we ev - er knew.

Additional Lyrics

2. Soft moonlight on your face,
   Oh, how you shine.
   It takes my breath away
   Just to look into your eyes.
   I know I don't deserve
   A treasure like you.
   There really are no words
   To show my gratitude.
   So, I tip my hat...

Killing Floor

Words and Music by Chester Burnett

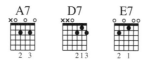

Strum Pattern: 1
Pick Pattern: 2

I should-'ve quit you long — time a - go. —
Instrumental

I should-'ve quit you, ba - by, long — time a - go. — *Spoken: Yes, I*

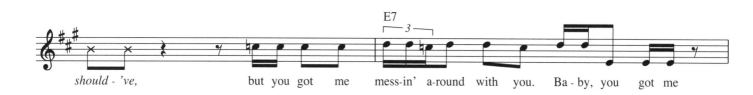

should - 've, but you got me mess-in' a-round with you. Ba - by, you got me

cry - in' — on the kill - ing floor. — If I'd have fol-lowed you

my first night, —— if I'd have fol-lowed, pret - ty ba - by,

my first night, _____ I would-'ve been gone

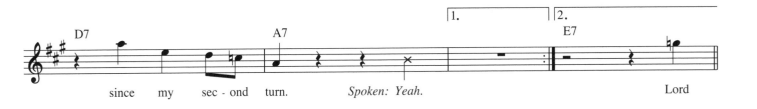

since my sec - ond turn. *Spoken: Yeah.* Lord

Outro

knows, _ Lord knows _ I should-'ve been gone.
Spoken: You got me hot.

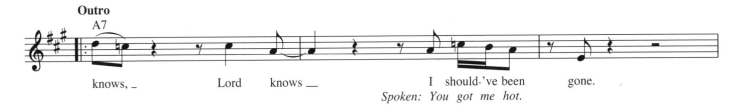

Lord knows, _____ I should-'ve been gone.
You got me hot. *Ooh.* *You got me on you, babe. Ooh*

She got me mess - in' a - round with you, ba - by, you got me

cry - in' ____ on the kill - ing floor. _ *Spoken: Uh!* *That's all.*

Money for Nothing

Words and Music by Mark Knopfler and Sting

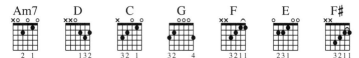

Strum Pattern: 2
Pick Pattern: 4

Intro
Moderate Rock

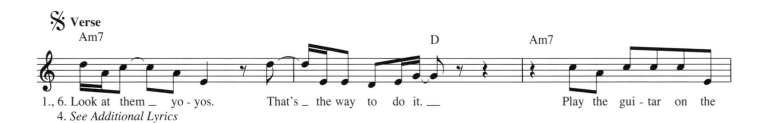

1., 6. Look at them _ yo - yos. That's _ the way to do it. _ Play the gui - tar on the
4. *See Additional Lyrics*

M.   T.   V.   That ain't _ work - in'. That's _ the way to do it.

Mon - ey for noth - in' and chicks for free. _   2. That ain't work - in'. That's _
3., 5. *See Additional Lyrics*

_ the way you do it.   Lem - me tell ya them _ guys ain't dumb. _

May - be get a blis - ter on your lit - tle fin - ger. May - be get a

Chorus

blis - ter on your __ thumb. __ We got - ta in - stall mi - cro - wave ov - ens,

cust - om kit - chen de - liv - er - ies. _____ We got - ta move these

2nd time, D.S.
3rd time, D.S. al Coda

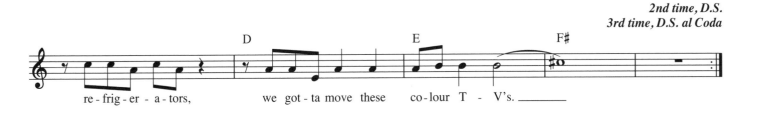

re - frig - er - a - tors, we got - ta move these co - lour T - V's. _____

Coda
Outro

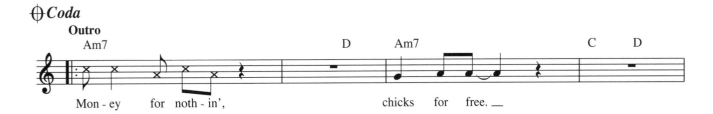

Mon - ey for noth - in', chicks for free. __

Repeat and Fade

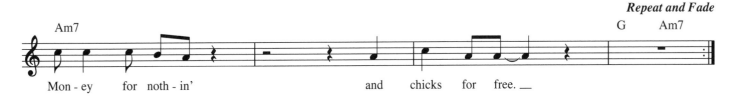

Mon - ey for noth - in' and chicks for free. __

Additional Lyrics

3. See that little faggot with the earring and the makeup.
   Yeah, buddy, that's his own hair.
   That little faggot got his own jet airplane.
   That little faggot he's a millionaire.

4. I shoulda learned to play the guitar.
   I shoulda learned to play them drums.
   Look at that, she got it stickin' in the camera.
   Man, we could have some fun.

5. And he's up there he's making Hawaiian noises,
   Bangin' on the the bongos like a chimpanzee.
   That ain't workin'. That's the way you do it.
   Money for nothin' and chicks for free.

Paranoid

Words and Music by Anthony Iommi, John Osbourne, William Ward and Terence Butler

Strum Pattern: 1
Pick Pattern: 2

Intro
Hard Rock

E5

Verse
E5

1. Fin - ished with __ my wom - an 'cause __ she
4. *See additional lyrics*

D5   G5   D5   E5

could - n't help __ me with my mind.   Peo - ple think __ I'm in -

D5   G5   D5   E5

- sane be - cause I am frown - ing all the time.

Interlude
E5   C5   D5   E5

Verse
E5   D5

2. All day long __ I think __ of things __ but noth - ing seems __ to
5. *See additional lyrics*

G5   D5   E5

sat - is - fy.   Think I'll lose __ my mind __ if I __ don't

Additional Lyrics

4. Make a joke and I will sigh
   And you will laugh and I will cry.
   Happiness I cannot feel
   And love to me is so unreal.

5. And so as you hear these words
   Telling you now of my state.
   I tell you to enjoy life,
   I wish I could but it's too late.

Through the Years

Words and Music by Steve Dorff and Marty Panzer

Strum Pattern: 3, 4
Pick Pattern: 5

Intro
Moderately, in 2

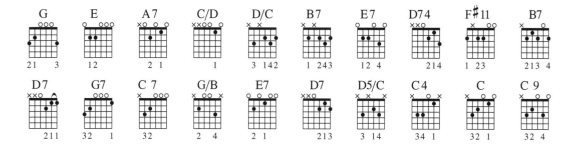

1. I

Verse

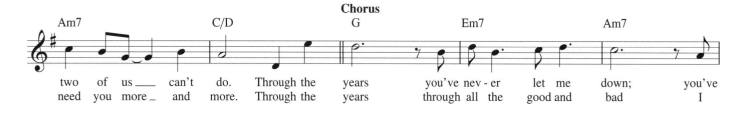

can't re-mem - ber when _ you were - n't there, _ when I did - n't care _ for
can't re-mem - ber what _ I used _ to do, _ who I trust - ed, who _ I

an - y - one _ but you. I swear _ we've been through ev - 'ry - thing _ there is. _
lis-tened to _ be - fore. I swear _ you've taught me ev - 'ry - thing _ I know _

_ Can't im - ag - ine an - y - thing _ we've missed. Can't im - ag - ine an - y - thing _ the
_ Can't im - ag - ine need - ing some - one so. But through the years it seems to me _ I

Chorus

two of us _ can't do. Through the years you've nev - er let me down; you've
need you more _ and more. Through the years through all the good and bad I

turned my life _ a - round. The sweet - est days _ I've found, I've found with
knew how much _ we _ had. I've al - ways been _ so glad to be with

We Gotta Get Out of This Place

Words and Music by Barry Mann and Cynthia Weil

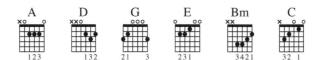

Strum Pattern: 6
Pick Pattern: 4

Verse
Moderately

In this dir-ty old part __ of the cit-y where the sun re-fuse __

__ to shine, __ peo-ple tell me there ain't __ no use __ in tryin'. __

__ My lit-tle girl, __ you're so young and __ pret-ty.

And one thing I know __ is true: __ you'll be dead be-fore __

__ your time is through. __ See my dad-dy in bed. __

__ He's dy-in'. You know his hair is turn-ing grey. __

He's been work-ing and slav - ing his life a - way. ____

Pre-Chorus

A

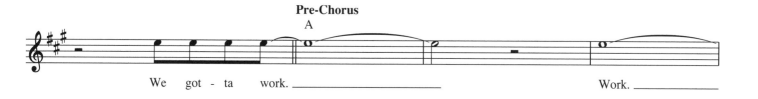

We got - ta work. _____ Work. _____

____ We got - ta work. _____ Work, work,

Chorus

D   G   A

work, work. We got - ta get out ____ of this place ____

D   E   A   D

if it's the last thing we ev - er do. ____ We got - ta get out ____

G   A   Bm

____ of this place. ____ Girl, there's a bet - ter life for me and you. ____

D   C   G   A   D   C   G   A

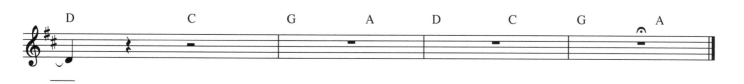

____

Wonderful Tonight

Words and Music by Eric Clapton

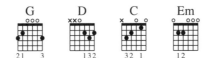

Strum Pattern: 4
Pick Pattern: 1

Intro
Moderately

1. It's late in the eve - ning; she's won-d'ring what clothes ___
2., 3. *See Additional Lyrics*

___ to wear. ___ She puts on her make - up and brush-es her long ___

___ blonde hair. ___ And then she asks ___ me, "Do I look all right?" ___

To Coda ⊕

___ And I say, "Yes, you look won - der - ful ___ to - night." ___

1.

Additional Lyrics

2. We go to a party, and ev'ryone turns to see.
   This beautiful lady is walking around with me.
   And then she asks me, "Do you feel alright?"
   And I say, "Yes, I feel wonderful tonight."

3. It's time to go home now, and I've got an aching head.
   So I give her the car keys, and she helps me to bed.
   And then I tell her, as I turn out the light,
   I say, "My darling, you are wonderful tonight."
   Oh, my darling, you are wonderful tonight.

The Thrill Is Gone

Words and Music by Roy Hawkins and Rick Darnell

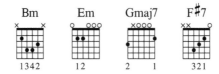

Strum Pattern: 1, 3
Pick Pattern: 2, 5
Verse
Moderately slow

1. The thrill is gone,__ the thrill is gone a - way.
2., 3., 4. *See additional lyrics*

The thrill is gone,__ ba - by, the thrill is gone

a - way. You know you done me wrong, ba -

- by, and you'll be sor - ry some - day._____

Additional Lyrics

2. The thrill is gone, it's gone away from me.
The thrill is gone, it's gone away from me.
Although I still live on,
But so lonely I'll be.

3. The thrill is gone, it's gone away for good.
The thrill is gone, it's gone away for good.
Someday I know I'll be over it all, baby,
Just like I know a good man should.

3. You know I'm free, free now, baby, I'm free from your spell.
I'm free, free, free now, I'm free from your spell.
And now that it's all over,
All I can do is wish you well.

Blue in Green

By Miles Davis

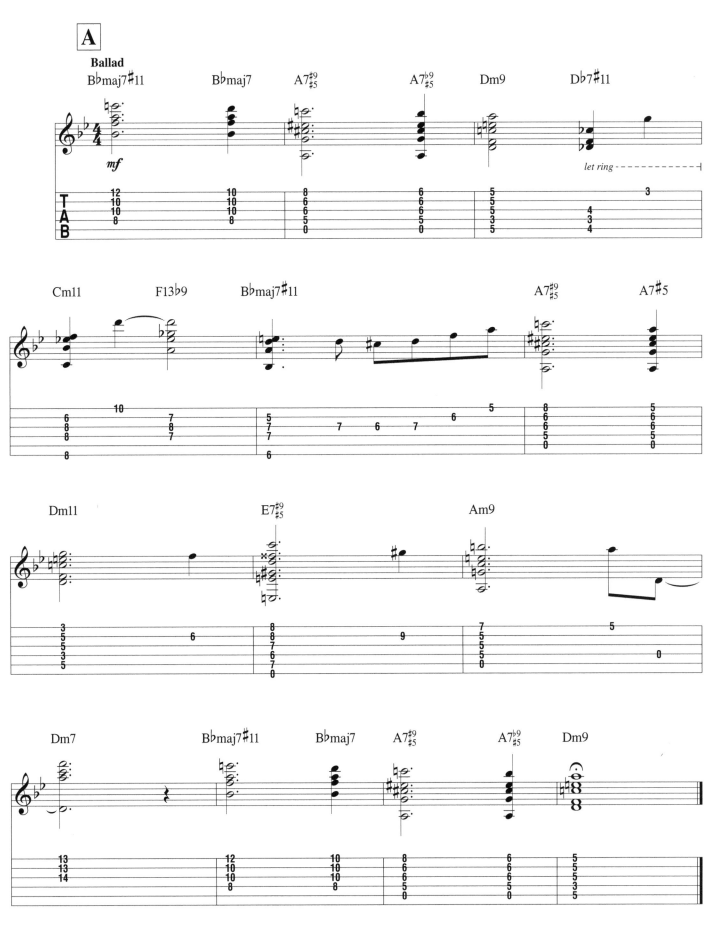

Detour Ahead

By Herb Ellis, John Frigo and Lou Carter

Lullaby of Birdland

Words by George David Weiss
Music by George Shearing

St. Thomas

By Sonny Rollins

Intro

Moderately fast Calypso

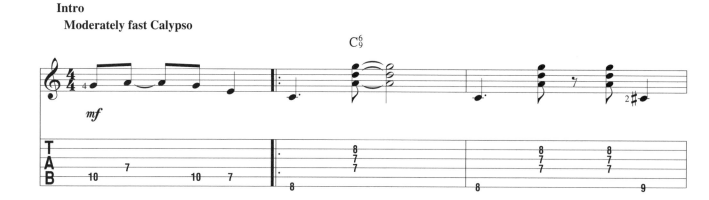

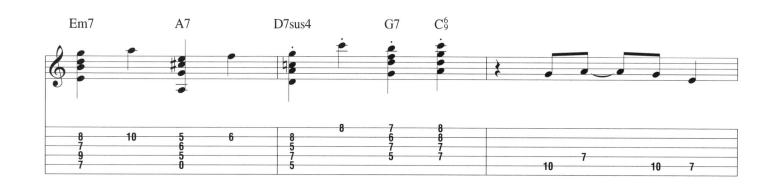

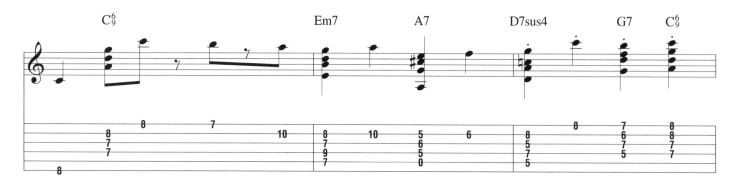

A Night in Tunisia

By John "Dizzy" Gillespie and Frank Paparelli

I'll Be Seeing You

from RIGHT THIS WAY

Written by Irving Kahal and Sammy Fain

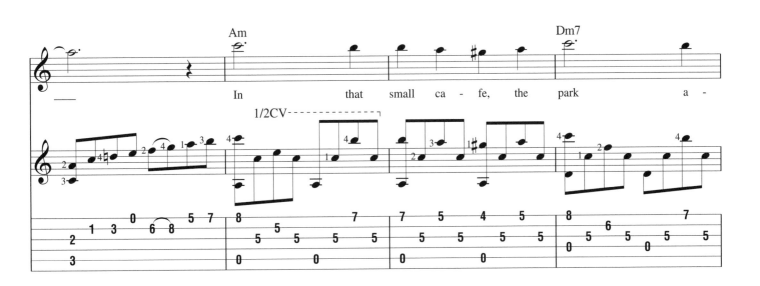

cross the way, the chil - dren's car-ou-sel, __ the chest-nut trees, __ the

wish-ing well. __ I'll be see - ing you in ev - 'ry love - ly

sum - mer's day, in ev - 'ry-thing that's light and gay. I'll al - ways think of

you   that way.   I'll   find   you   in   the   morn - ing sun.   And   when   the night is

new,   I'll be look-ing at the moon,_____ but I'll be see - ing   you!

you!_____

Do You Know Where You're Going To?

Theme from MAHOGANY
Words by Gerry Goffin
Music by Michael Masser

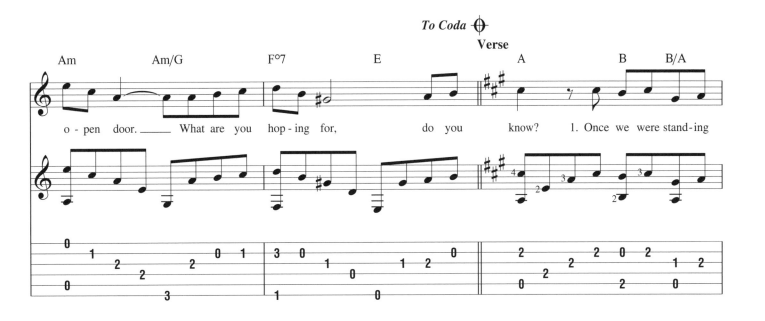

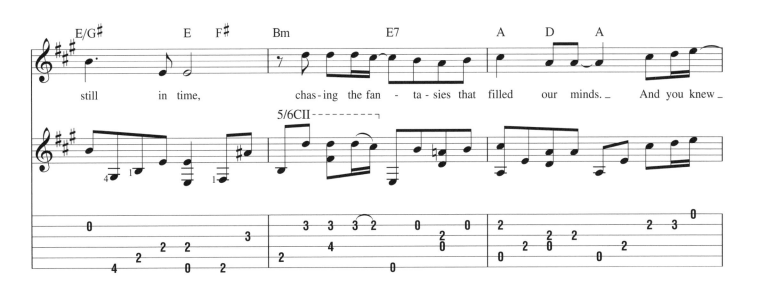

Chorus

once asked of me. Do you know _____ where you're go - ing to?

Do you like the things that life is show-ing you? _____ Where are you go-ing to, do you know?

Interlude

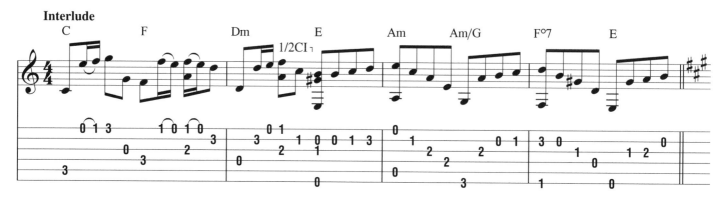

Verse

2. Now look-ing back at all we planned, we let so man - y dreams just

slip through our hands. ___ Why must ___ we wait so long ___ be - fore we see

D.C. al Coda

how sad the an-swers to those ques-tions can be?

$\oplus$ **Coda**

Outro

know?

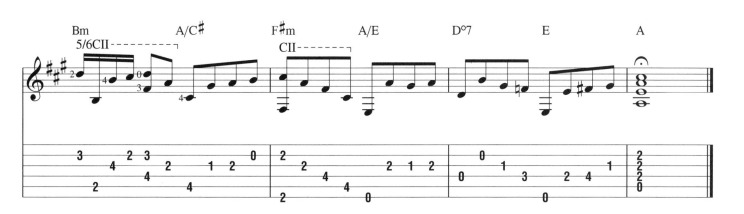

Duelin' Banjos

By Arthur Smith

*To imitate banjo, pick near bridge where indicated by asterisk.

strum sim. throughout

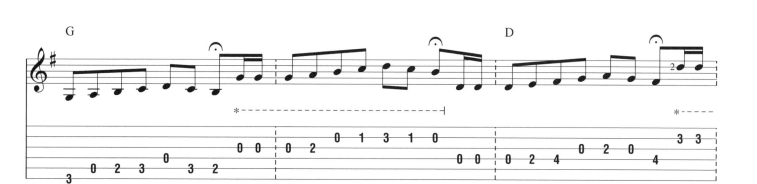

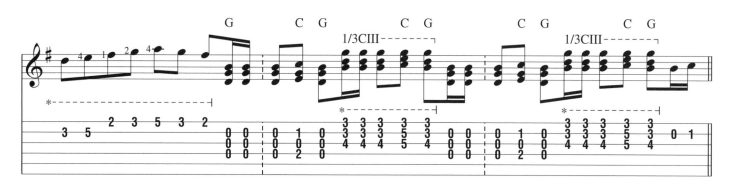

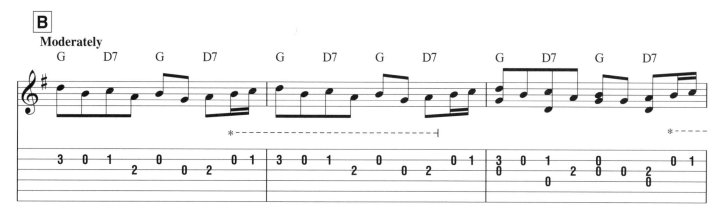

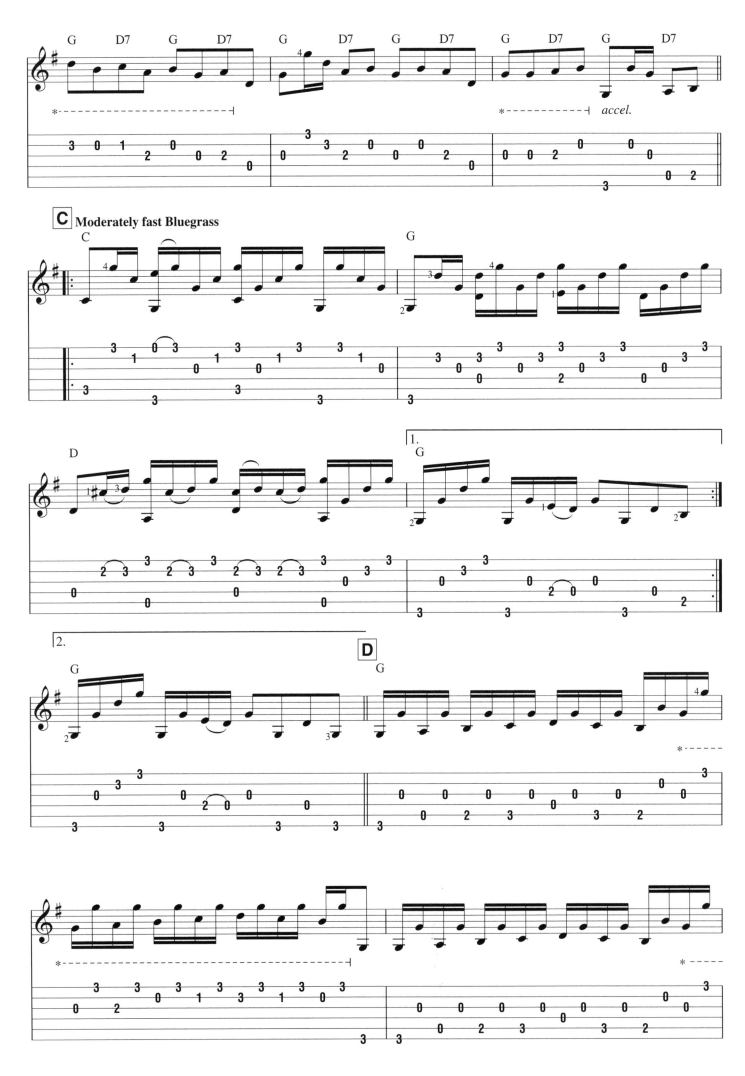

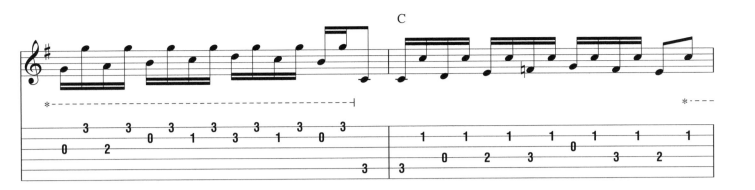

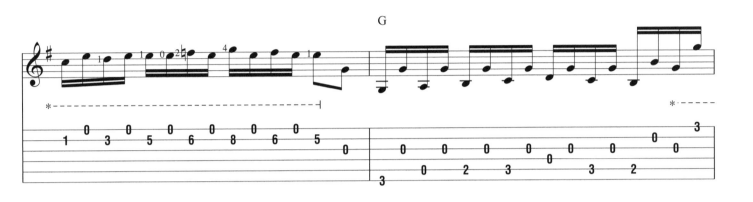

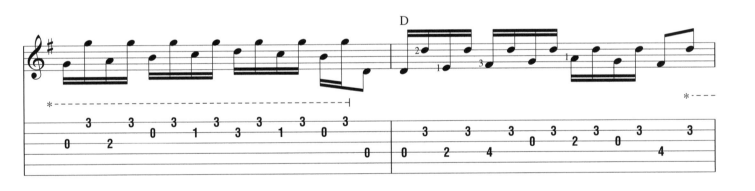

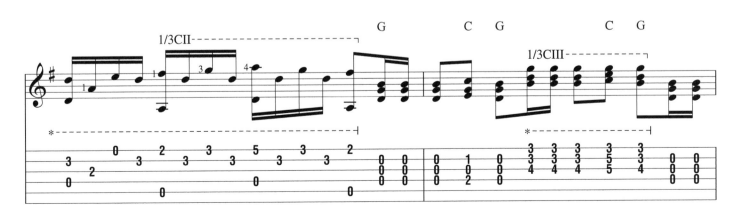

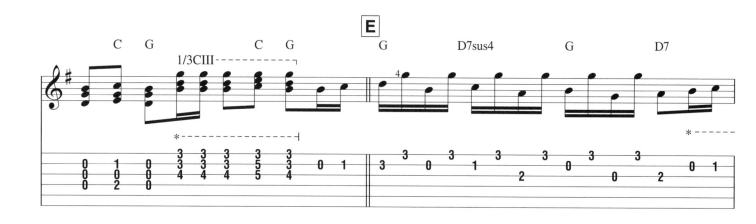

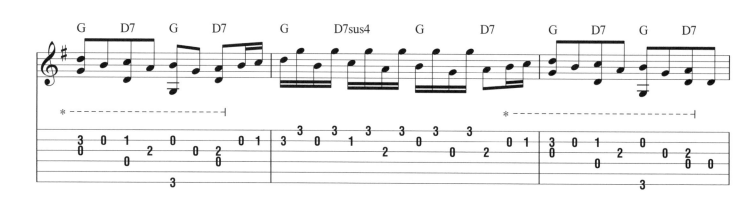

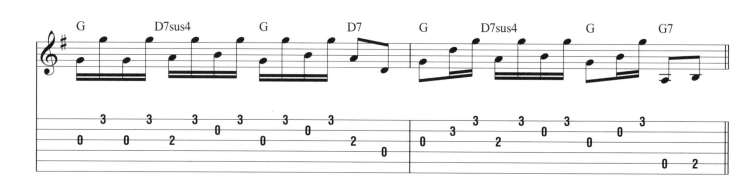

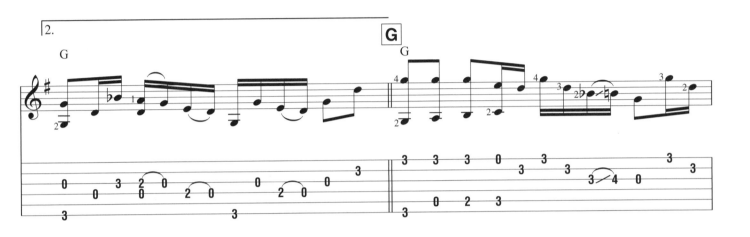

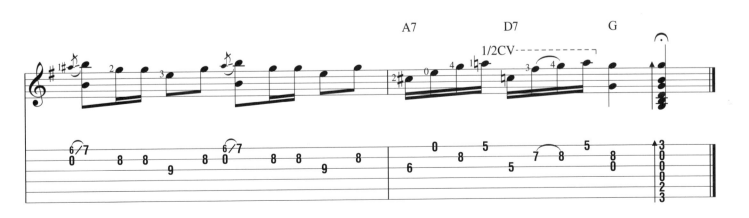

I'd Love to Change the World

Words and Music by Alvin Lee

201

Additional Lyrics

2. Population keeps on breeding.
   Nation bleeding, still more feeding economy.
   Life is funny; skies are sunny.
   Bees make honey; who needs money?
   Monopoly.
   No, not for me.

Knockin' on Heaven's Door

Words and Music by Bob Dylan

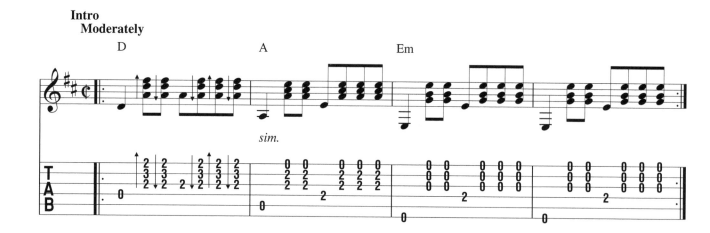

1. Ma-ma, take this badge off of me. ____
2., 3. *See additional lyrics*

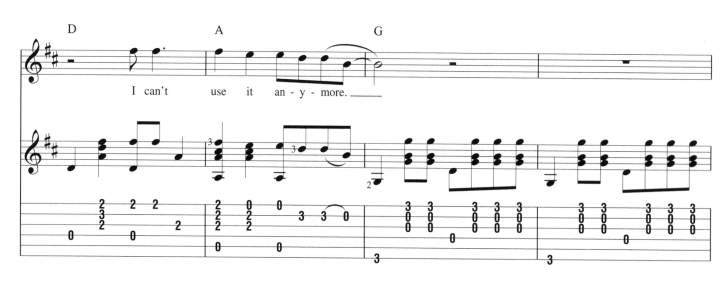

I can't use it an-y-more. ____

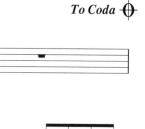

Knock, knock, knock-in' on heav-en's door.

1.

Just like so man-y times be - fore.

2.

D.S. al Coda

Just like so man-y times be - fore.

Coda

Just like so man-y times be - fore. _____

Outro

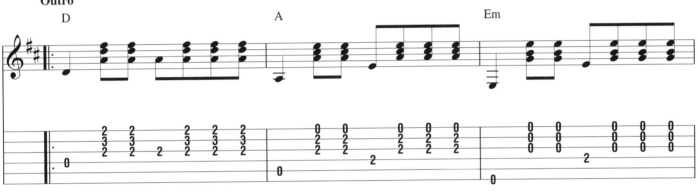

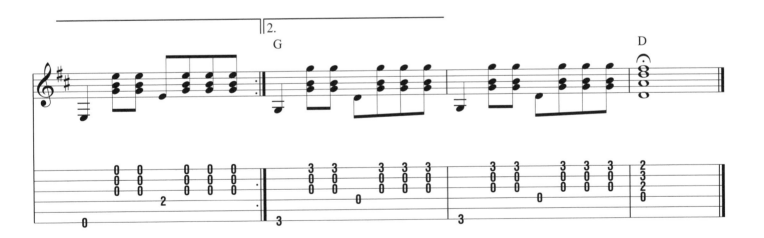

Additional Lyrics

2. Mama, wipe the blood out of my face.
   I just can't see through it anymore.
   Got a long black feelin' and it's hard to trace,
   And I feel like I'm knockin' on heaven's door.

3. Mama, lay them guns onto the ground.
   I just can't fire them anymore.
   That long black cape is pulling on down,
   And I feel like I' knockin' on heaven's door.

Seasons of Love

from RENT

Words and Music by Jonathan Larson

Five hun-dred twen-ty-five thou-sand six hun-dred min - utes. How do you meas-ure the life of a

wom - an or a man? In truth that she learned or in times that he cried, __ in

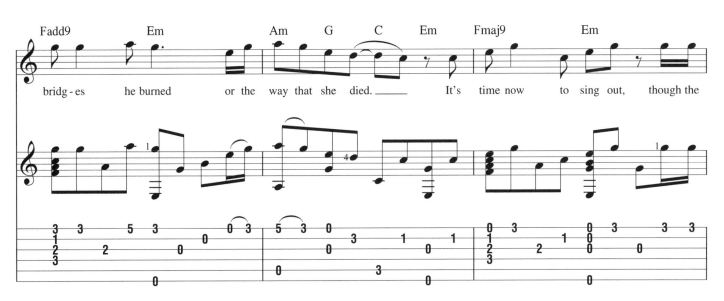

bridg-es he burned or the way that she died. _____ It's time now to sing out, though the

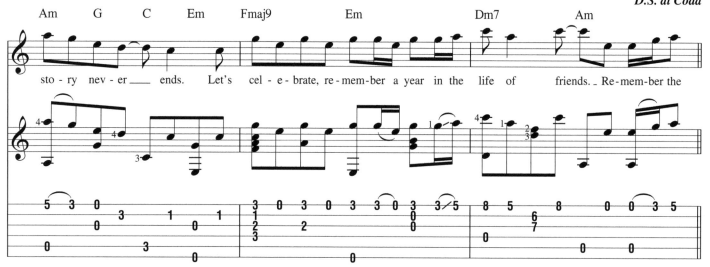

Coda

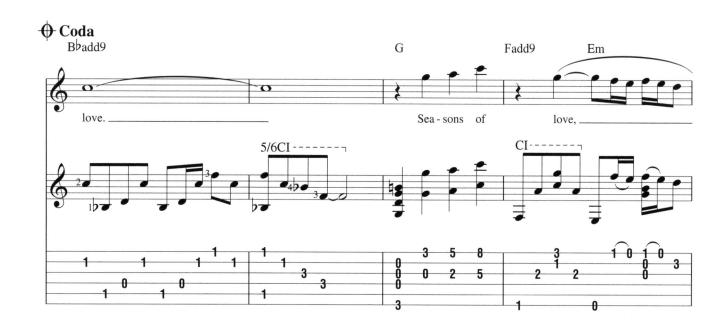

Arabian Dance

("Coffee")

from THE NUTCRACKER
By Pyotr Il'yich Tchaikovsky

Tuning:
(low to high) E-B-E-G-B-E

Moderately fast

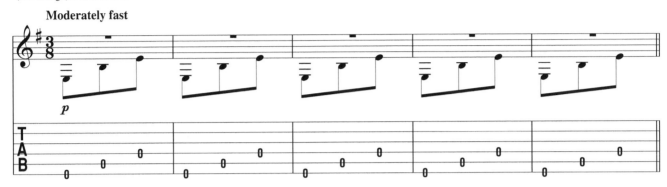

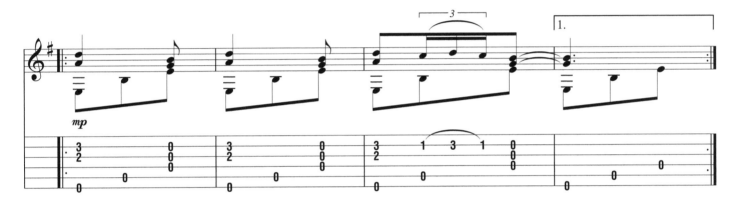

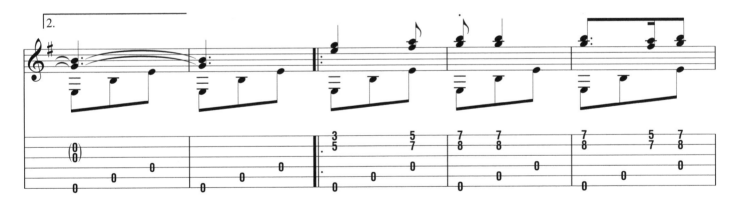

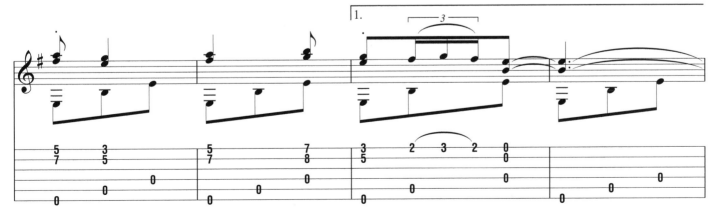

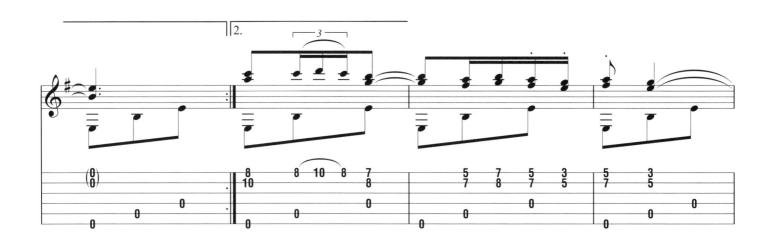

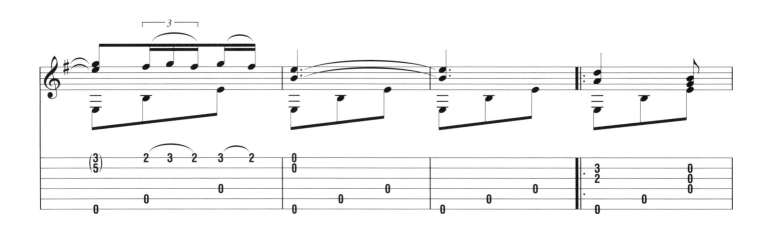

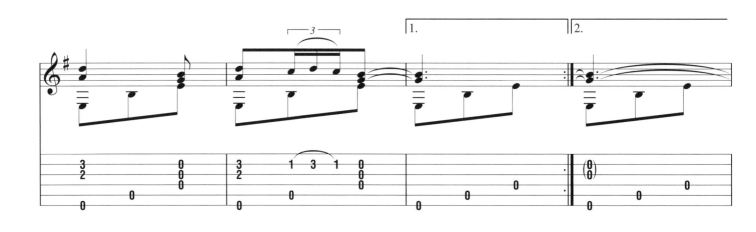

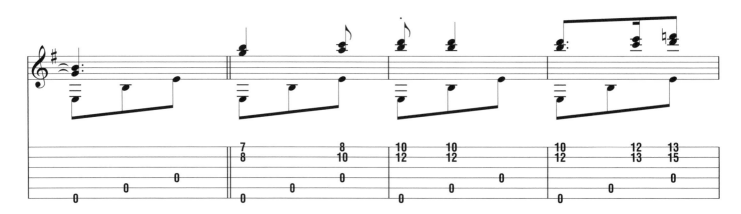

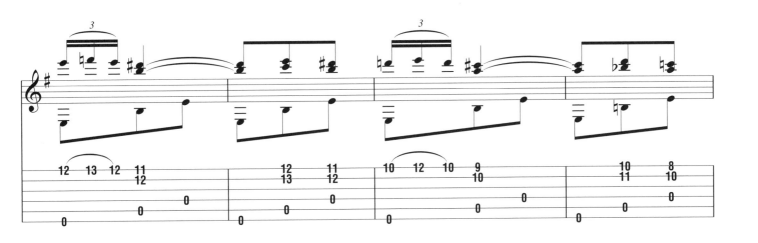

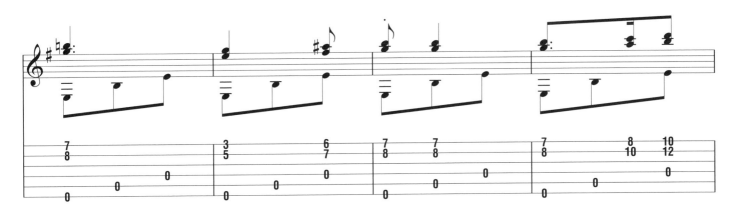

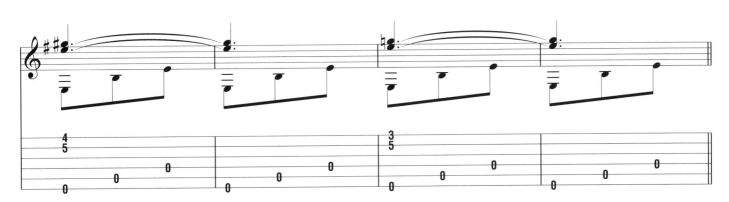

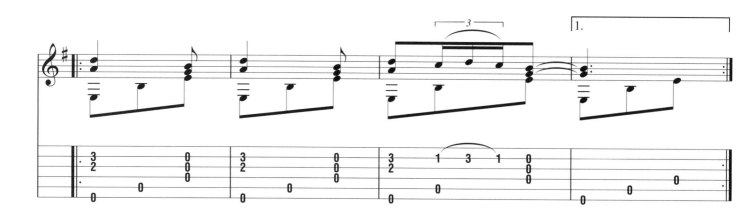

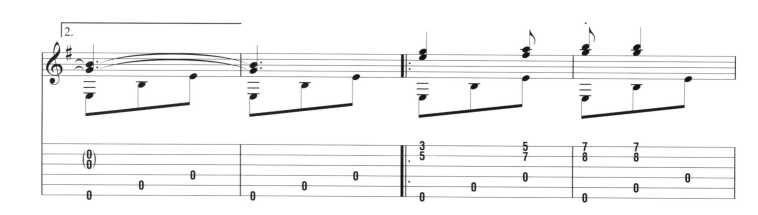

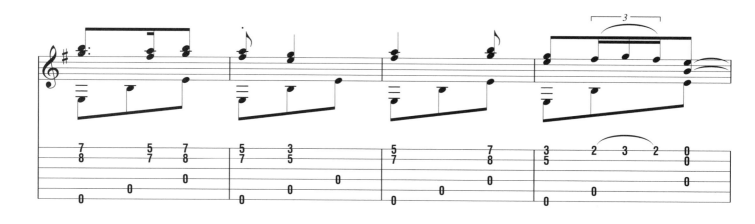

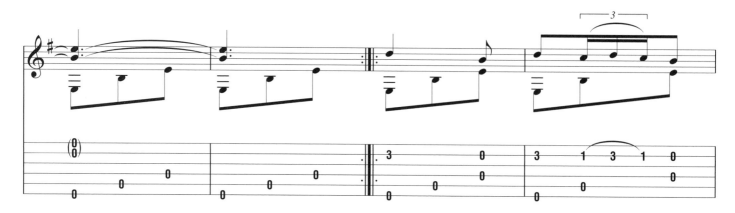

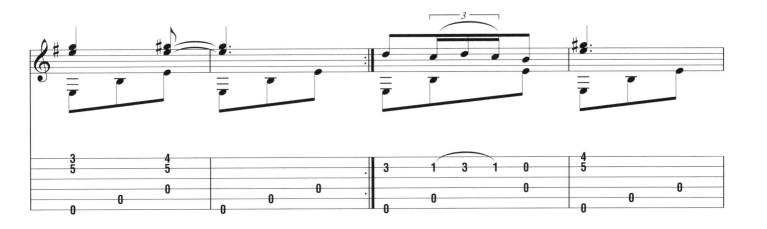

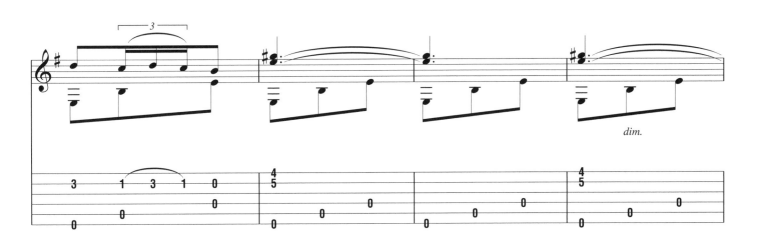

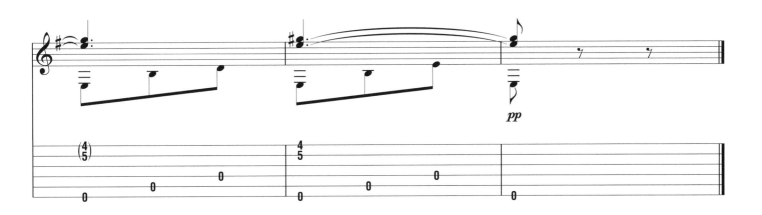

Caro Mio Ben

Text from an Anonymous Italian poem
Music by Tommaso Giordani

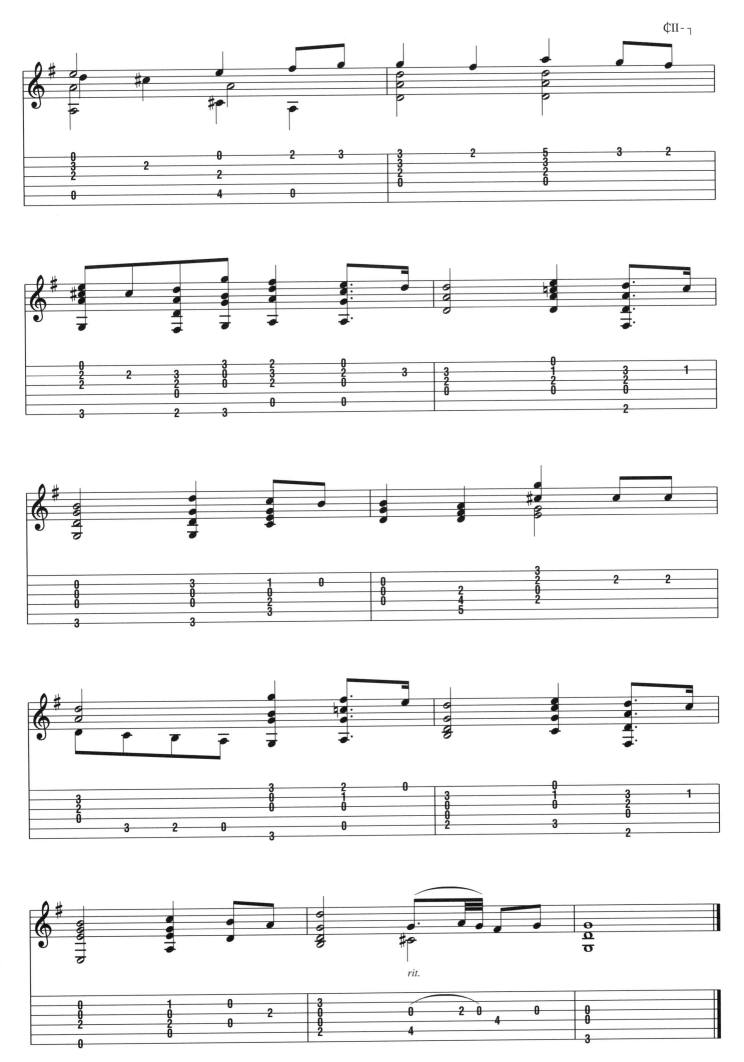

Evening Prayer

from HANSEL AND GRETEL
By Engelbert Humperdinck

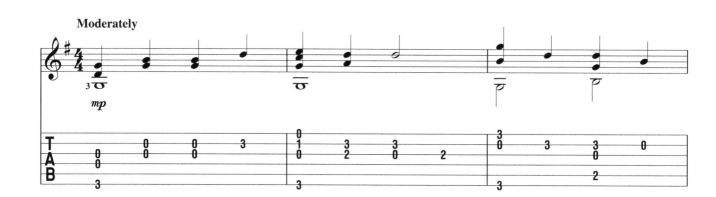

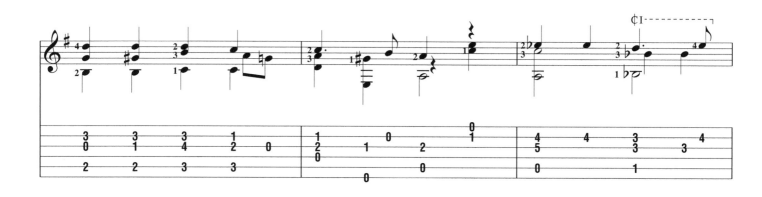

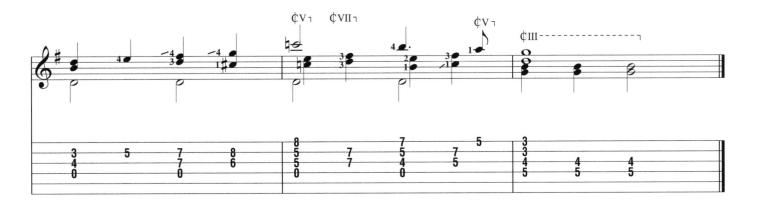

Panis Angelicus
(O Lord Most Holy)

By Cesar Franck

Moderately slow

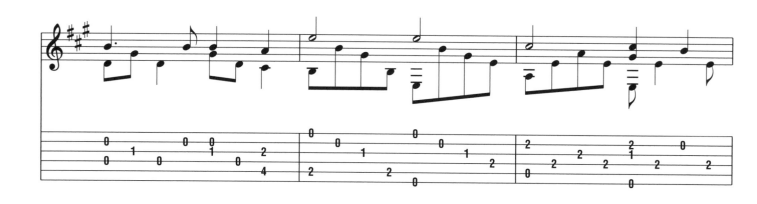

223

Sleepers, Awake
(Wachet Auf)
from CANTATA NO. 140
By Johann Sebastian Bach

Drop D tuning:
(low to high) D-A-D-G-B-E

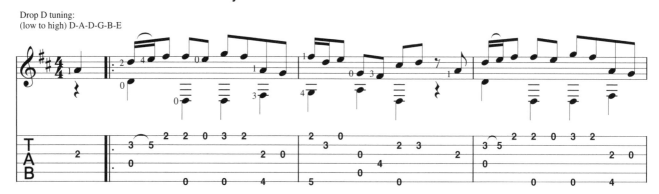

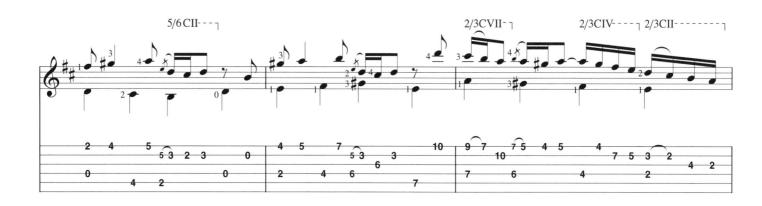

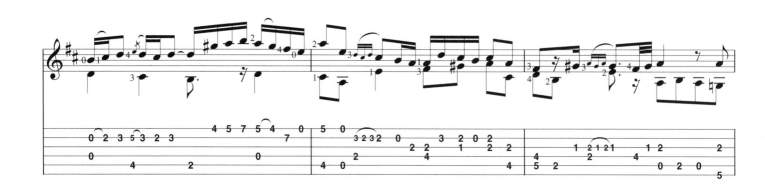

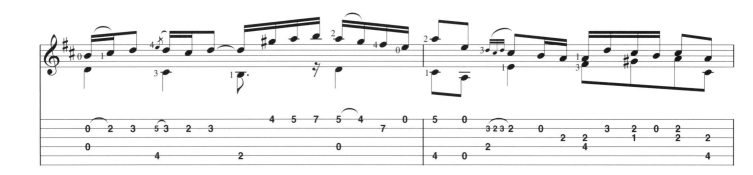

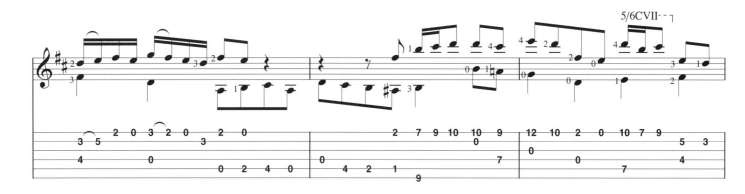

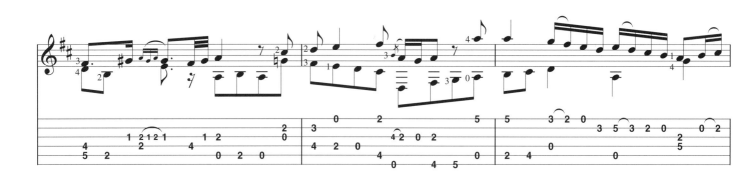

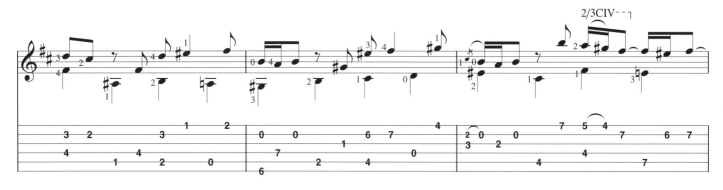

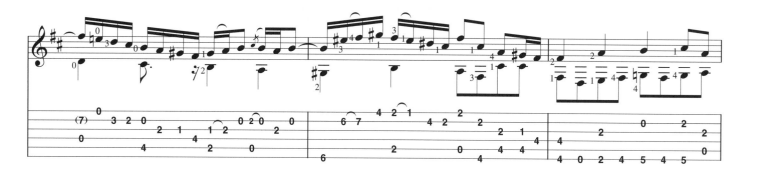

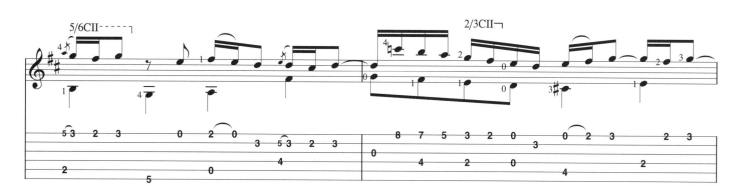

Pie Jesu

By Gabriel Fauré

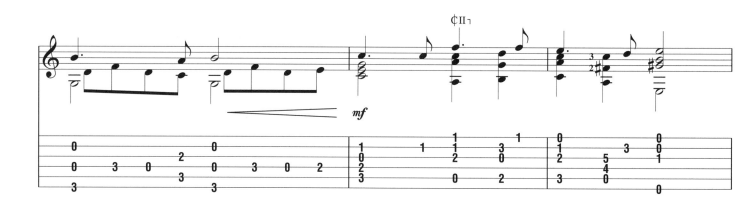

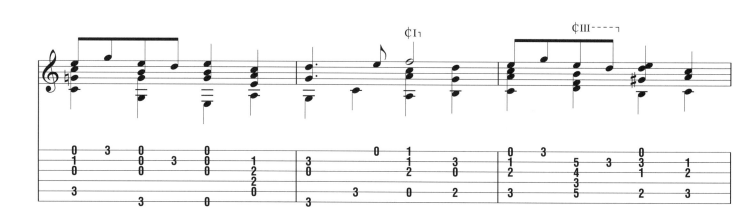

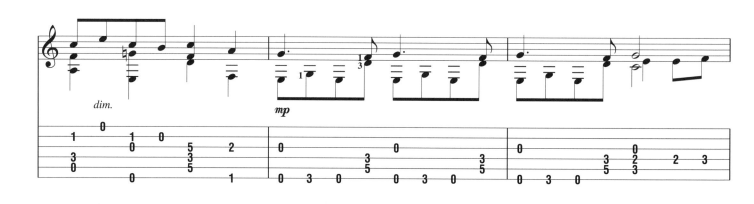

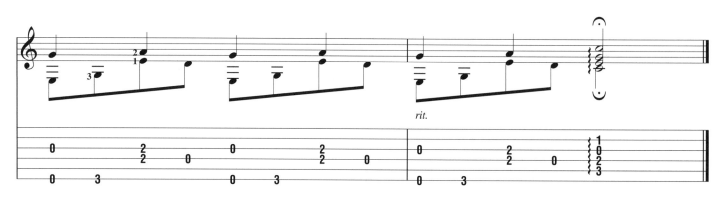

Back in Black

Words and Music by Angus Young, Malcolm Young and Brian Johnson

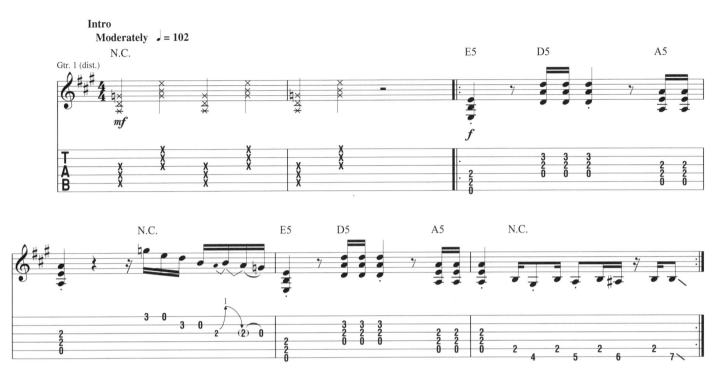

Been Caught Stealing

Words and Music by Jane's Addiction

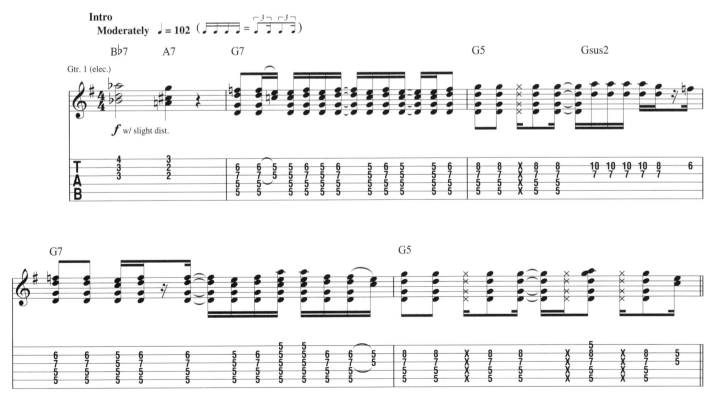

Birthday

Words and Music by John Lennon and Paul McCartney

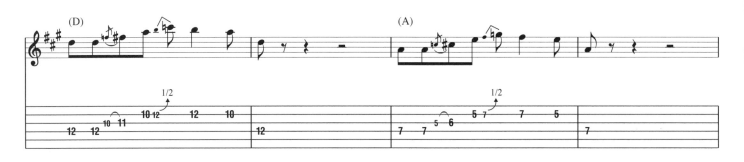

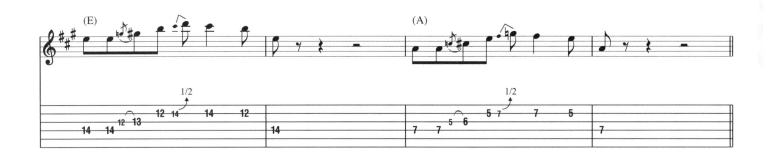

Breaking the Law

Words and Music by Glenn Tipton, Rob Halford and K.K. Downing

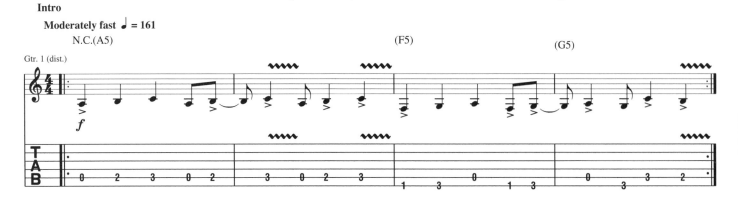

The Bleeding

Words and Music by Ivan Moody and Zoltan Bathory

Tune down 2 1/2 steps:
(low to high) B-E-A-D-F#-C

Intro
Moderately slow ♩ = 70

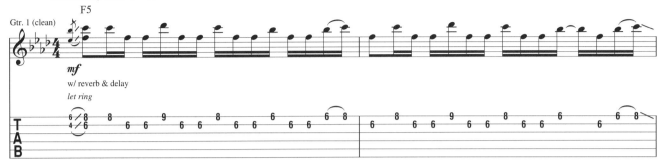

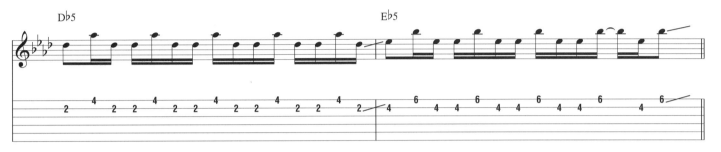

Sultans of Swing

Words and Music by Mark Knopfler

Intro
Moderately ♩ =146

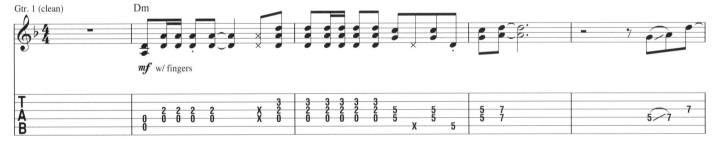

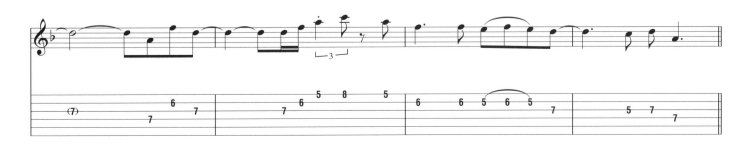

Divinations

Words and Music by Brann Dailor, William Hinds, William Kelliher and Troy Sanders

Tune down 1 step:
(low to high) D-G-C-F-A-D

La Grange

Words and Music by Billy F Gibbons, Dusty Hill and Frank Lee Beard

*Chord symbols reflect basic harmony.

One Step Closer

Words and Music by Rob Bourdon, Brad Delson, Joe Hahn, Mike Shinoda and Charles Bennington

Drop D tuning, down 1/2 step:
(low to high) Db-Ab-Db-Gb-Bb-Eb

Intro

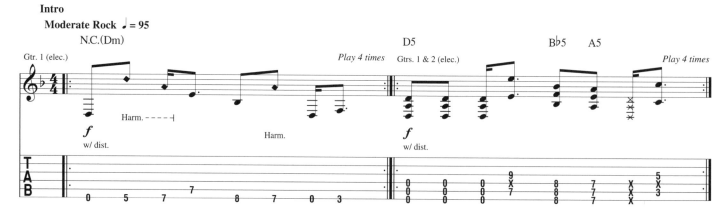

Just Like Heaven

Words and Music by Robert Smith, Laurence Tolhurst, Simon Gallup, Paul S. Thompson and Boris Williams

*Delay set for quarter-note regeneration w/ 1 repeat.

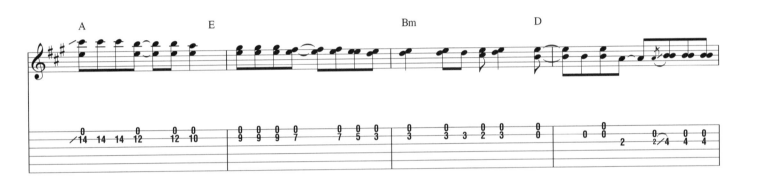

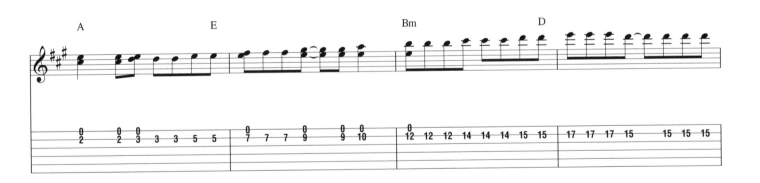

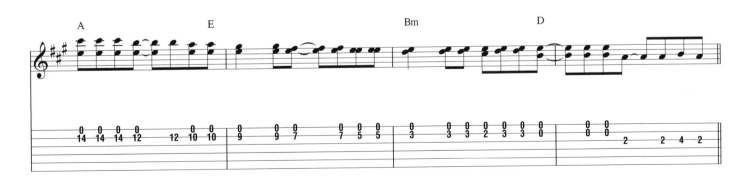

Outshined

Words and Music by Chris Cornell

Drop D tuning:
(low to high) D-A-D-G-B-E

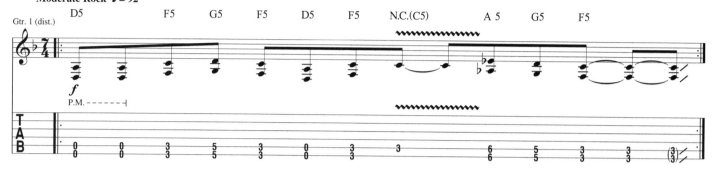

Raining Blood

Words and Music by Jeff Hanneman and Kerry King

Tune down 1/2 step:
(low to high) Eb-Ab-Db-Gb-Bb-Eb

Runnin' with the Devil

Words and Music by David Lee Roth, Edward Van Halen, Alex Van Halen and Michael Anthony

Tune down 1/2 step:
(low to high) Eb-Ab-Db-Gb-Bb-Eb

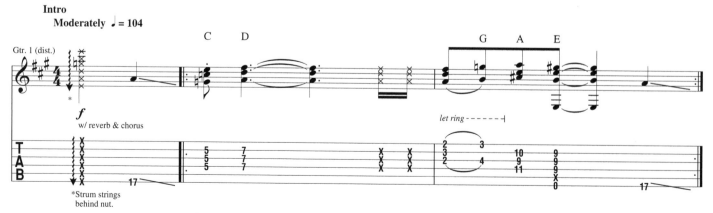

Take Me Out

Words and Music by Alex Kapranos and Nick McCarthy

The Trooper

Words and Music by Steven Harris

*Chord symbols refelect overall harmony.

Who Do You Love

Words and Music by Ellas McDaniel

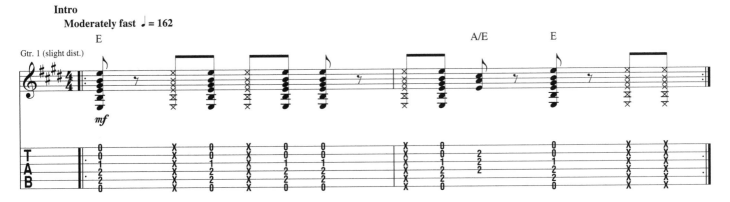

GUITAR NOTATION LEGEND

Guitar music can be notated three different ways: on a *musical staff*, in *tablature*, and in *rhythm slashes*.

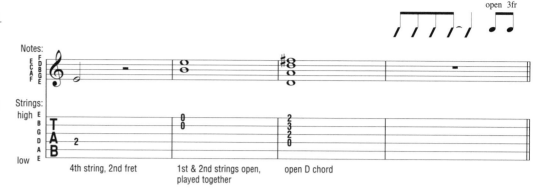

RHYTHM SLASHES are written above the staff. Strum chords in the rhythm indicated. Use the chord diagrams found at the top of the first page of the transcription for the appropriate chord voicings. Round noteheads indicate single notes.

THE MUSICAL STAFF shows pitches and rhythms and is divided by bar lines into measures. Pitches are named after the first seven letters of the alphabet.

TABLATURE graphically represents the guitar fingerboard. Each horizontal line represents a string, and each number represents a fret.

4th string, 2nd fret

1st & 2nd strings open, played together

open D chord

HALF-STEP BEND: Strike the note and bend up 1/2 step.

WHOLE-STEP BEND: Strike the note and bend up one step.

GRACE NOTE BEND: Strike the note and immediately bend up as indicated.

SLIGHT (MICROTONE) BEND: Strike the note and bend up 1/4 step.

BEND AND RELEASE: Strike the note and bend up as indicated, then release back to the original note. Only the first note is struck.

PRE-BEND: Bend the note as indicated, then strike it.

VIBRATO: The string is vibrated by rapidly bending and releasing the note with the fretting hand.

WIDE VIBRATO: The pitch is varied to a greater degree by vibrating with the fretting hand.

HAMMER-ON: Strike the first (lower) note with one finger, then sound the higher note (on the same string) with another finger by fretting it without picking.

PULL-OFF: Place both fingers on the notes to be sounded. Strike the first note and without picking, pull the finger off to sound the second (lower) note.

LEGATO SLIDE: Strike the first note and then slide the same fret-hand finger up or down to the second note. The second note is not struck.

SHIFT SLIDE: Same as legato slide, except the second note is struck.

TRILL: Very rapidly alternate between the notes indicated by continuously hammering on and pulling off.

TAPPING: Hammer ("tap") the fret indicated with the pick-hand index or middle finger and pull off to the note fretted by the fret hand.

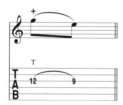

NATURAL HARMONIC: Strike the note while the fret-hand lightly touches the string directly over the fret indicated.

PINCH HARMONIC: The note is fretted normally and a harmonic is produced by adding the edge of the thumb or the tip of the index finger of the pick hand to the normal pick attack.

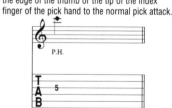

PICK SCRAPE: The edge of the pick is rubbed down (or up) the string, producing a scratchy sound.

MUFFLED STRINGS: A percussive sound is produced by laying the fret hand across the string(s) without depressing, and striking them with the pick hand.

PALM MUTING: The note is partially muted by the pick hand lightly touching the string(s) just before the bridge.

RAKE: Drag the pick across the strings indicated with a single motion.

TREMOLO PICKING: The note is picked as rapidly and continuously as possible.

VIBRATO BAR DIVE AND RETURN: The pitch of the note or chord is dropped a specified number of steps (in rhythm), then returned to the original pitch.

VIBRATO BAR SCOOP: Depress the bar just before striking the note, then quickly release the bar.

VIBRATO BAR DIP: Strike the note and then immediately drop a specified number of steps, then release back to the original pitch.

STRUM AND PICK PATTERNS

This chart contains the suggested strum and pick patterns that are referred to by number at the beginning of each song in this book. The symbols ⊓ and ∨ in the strum patterns refer to down and up strokes, respectively. The letters in the pick patterns indicate which right-hand fingers play which strings.

p = thumb
i = index finger
m = middle finger
a = ring finger

For example; Pick Pattern 2
is played: thumb - index - middle - ring

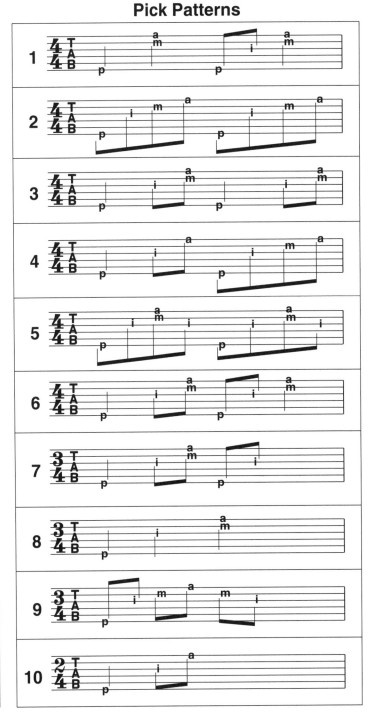

You can use the 3/4 Strum and Pick Patterns in songs written in compound meter (6/8, 9/8, 12/8, etc.).
For example, you can accompany a song in 6/8 by playing the 3/4 pattern twice in each measure.
The 4/4 Strum and Pick Patterns can be used for songs written in cut time (¢) by doubling the note time values in the patterns. Each pattern would therefore last two measures in cut time.

Must-Have Collections for Every Guitarist!

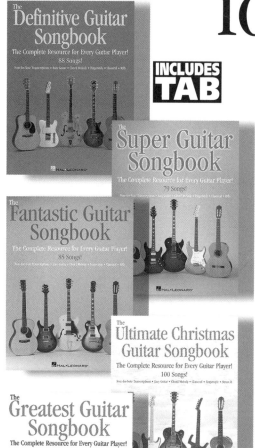

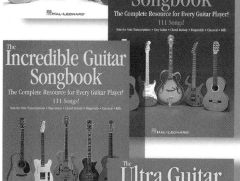

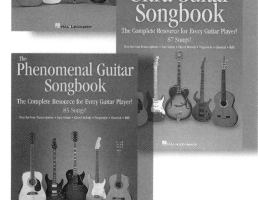

The Definitive Guitar Songbook

There's something for every guitarist in this amazing collection! It features 88 songs in all styles of music and all forms of notation, including: Guitar Recorded Versions (Birthday • Ramblin' Man); Easy Guitar with Notes & Tab (Blackbird • Don't Be Cruel); Easy Guitar (Baby Love • Cheek to Cheek • Young Americans); Chord Melody Guitar (I Could Write a Book • When I Fall in Love); Classical Guitar (Gavotte • Prelude); Fingerstyle Guitar (Imagine • My One and Only Love); and Guitar Riffs (Fire and Rain • Maggie May • Twist and Shout).
00699267 Guitar Collection $19.95

The Fantastic Guitar Songbook

85 tunes in a wide variety of notation formats (easy guitar with and without tablature, chord melody guitar, classical, fingerstyle, riffs and note-for-note tab transcriptions), and in a range of musical styles – from pop/rock hits to jazz standards, movie songs to Motown, country, classical and everything in between. Includes: ABC • Canon in D • Drops of Jupiter • Hey Jude • I Am a Man of Constant Sorrow • Jack and Diane • Leader of the Band • Mama, I'm Coming Home • Summer of '69 • So Nice (Summer Samba) • Tush • We've Only Just Begun • Yellow Submarine • and more.
00699561 Guitar Collection $19.95

The Greatest Guitar Songbook

This comprehensive collection for all guitarists includes 100 songs in genres from jazz standards, to pop/rock favorites, Motown masterpieces and movie music, to traditional tunes, country numbers and classical pieces. Notation styles include: note-for-note transcriptions (Sweet Child O' Mine • Wild Thing); Easy Guitar with Notes & Tab (Day Tripper • Für Elise • Misty); Easy Guitar (Boot Scootin' Boogie • Unchained Melody); Fingerstyle Guitar (Amazing Grace • Greensleeves); and Guitar Riffs (Angie • Layla • My Girl); and more!
00699142 Guitar Collection $20.95

The Incredible Guitar Songbook

Features a whopping 111 songs in genres from blues to jazz to pop and rock to classical and country, and a variety of notation styles, including: Note-for-note transcriptions in notes and tab (Tears in Heaven • Wonderwall); Easy Guitar with Notes and Tab (All Shook Up • Bésame Mucho • Pride and Joy); Easy Guitar, No Tab (Michelle • Route 66); Chord Melody Guitar (Satin Doll); Classical Guitar (Bourée • Pavane); Fingerstyle Guitar (Something); and Guitar Riffs (Beast of Burden • Gloria).
00699245 Guitar Collection $19.95

The Phenomenal Guitar Songbook

This remarkable book features 85 songs from all styles of music. It includes a variety of note-for-note transcriptions, riffs, and arrangements for easy guitar, chord melody, fingerstyle, and classical guitar. Songs include: Ain't Too Proud to Beg • Blue Skies • California Dreamin' • Fly like an Eagle • Fur Elise • Giant Steps • God Bless the U.S.A. • Good Vibrations • Green Onions • In My Life • Moon River • My Way • Proud Mary • Redneck Woman • Under the Bridge • What's Going On • You Are My Sunshine • and more!
00699759 Guitar Collection $19.99

The Super Guitar Songbook

The latest songbook in our wildly popular series of mixed collections of guitar arrangements and transcriptions. This book features 79 songs in a wide variety of music styles and notation formats: Guitar Recorded Versions, fingerstyle, easy guitar with notes and tab, classical, chord melody, and riffs! These books truly grow with the player! Songs include: Bewitched • California Girls • Come to My Window • (Everything I Do) I Do It for You • In a Sentimental Mood • Lucy in the Sky with Diamonds • Oye Como Va • Rocky Top • Scuttle Buttin' • Sharp Dressed Man • Soul Man • You'll Be in My Heart • and more!
00699618 Guitar Collection $19.99

The Ultimate Christmas Guitar Songbook

100 songs in a variety of notation styles, from easy guitar and classical guitar arrangements to note-for-note guitar tab transcriptions. Includes: All Through the Night • Auld Lang Syne • Blue Christmas • The Chipmunk Song • The Gift • (There's No Place Like) Home for the Holidays • I've Got My Love to Keep Me Warm • Jingle Bells • My Favorite Things • One Bright Star • Rockin' Around the Christmas Tree • Santa Baby • Silver Bells • Wonderful Christmastime • and more.
00700185 Guitar Collection $19.95

The Ultimate Guitar Songbook – Second Edition

110 songs in all genres and guitar styles: everything from pop/rock hits to jazz standards, Motown masterpieces to movie classics, traditional tunes, country favorites, Broadway blockbusters and beyond! Features note-for-note transcriptions, riffs, and arrangements for easy guitar, chord melody, fingerstyle, classical & more!
00699909 Guitar Collection $19.99

The Ultra Guitar Songbook

The latest edition in our popular series featuring multiple notation styles, perfect for players looking for a little variety in their playing! This collection features 87 songs in Guitar Recorded Versions notation (Bad Moon Rising • Hot for Teacher); Easy Guitar (Bennie and the Jets • Free Fallin' • Ring of Fire • Tainted Love); Chord Melody Guitar (Come Fly with Me • Witchcraft); Classical Guitar (Capricho Arabe • Minuet in G); Fingerstyle Guitar (Every Rose Has Its Thorn • Fields of Gold); Guitar Riffs (Beautiful Girls • Dancing with Myself); and many more!
00700130 Guitar Collection $19.95

Prices, contents, and availability subject to change without notice.

FOR MORE INFORMATION, SEE YOUR LOCAL MUSIC DEALER, OR WRITE TO:

HAL•LEONARD® CORPORATION
7777 W. BLUEMOUND RD. P.O. BOX 13819 MILWAUKEE, WI 53213

www.halleonard.com